Photography Business Basics

Photography Business Basics

A Professional Photographer's Guide to Financial Success

Written by Natasha Martinez with
Mark Maryanovich

BEP
BUSINESS EXPERT PRESS
Leader in applied, concise business books

Photography Business Basics:
A Professional Photographer's Guide to Financial Success

First published in 2025 by
Business Expert Press, LLC
222 East 46th Street, New York, NY 10017
www.businessexpertpress.com

ISBN-13: 978-1-63742-831-3 (paperback)
ISBN-13: 978-1-63742-832-0 (e-book)

Business Expert Press Business Career Development Collection

First edition: 2025

10 9 8 7 6 5 4 3 2 1

EU SAFETY REPRESENTATIVE
Mare Nostrum Group B.V.
Mauritskade 21D
1091 GC Amsterdam
The Netherlands
gpsr@mare-nostrum.co.uk

Description

Why do some photographers succeed when others fail? It's often because the successful ones know the *Photography Business Basics*.

Photography Business Basics is a current resource for emerging, mid-career, and experienced photographers of all specialties interested in starting or making their own freelance business the best it can be.

Written with a friendly, conversational tone, *Photography Business Basics* offers easy-to-read, practical advice explained in a step-by-step direction, using an innovative work-back plan that logically deconstructs a mountain of activities into smaller manageable actions.

You will learn how to:

- Determine goals that encompass your definition of Success
- Apply bookkeeping and accounting Fundamentals
- Implement the simple and most effective way to set your Pricing
- Create your Target Market Personas
- Design your Brand
- Craft your Sales Funnel
- Construct a Marketing Plan based on Marketing Math
- Use current SEO Strategies to improve your search engine rankings and discover the only analytics metric that matters
- Deliver a Client Experience that generates repeat business and referrals (the best and most profitable business you can have as a photographer)
- Build a solid Business Plan that lays the groundwork for success

Most photographers are creative by nature and lack the business skills and mindset needed to consistently earn a living as a Professional. Don't let this be you!

If you are overworked and underpaid and looking for a simple method to manage your business and earn more money then don't delay—read *Photography Business Basics*. Start building the most successful photography business you can today!

Contents

List of Images, Tables, and Figures

10 Elements of Professional Images

Figures

Tables

Review Quotes

"*Photography Business Basics is a book that would have helped me greatly as a young photographer. I learned how to be an artist first, which was fine, but I struggled with the business end of photography. Many wasted years! As I was going through this book I thought to myself that business instruction is so lacking in our industry. Look through hundreds of photography YouTube videos, for example, and you will find that only a few even touch on the business end of things. This needs to change, which is why Natasha and Mark's invaluable book is perfectly timed. Our industry is advancing and shifting rapidly, and my advice is to use this book as a solid foundation. Good business practices will help you get paid for doing the thing you love to do!*"—**Mark Hemmings, Photographer, Educator, Author of** *iPhone Photography For Dummies* **and** *Android Smartphone Photography For Dummies*, **https://markhemmings.com**

"*It's a no-brainer for any photographer new to business. Incredible book, I do mean that. It's well written, it's easy to digest and easy to read .... It goes into the basic details you need to run a successful business. The whole book is a very, very worthwhile investment.*"—**Andrew Hellmich, PhotoBizX Podcast, https://photobizx.com**

"*Photography Business Basics is packed with helpful tips for both new photographers and seasoned photographers wanting to turn their passion into a profit. As a CPA, I especially enjoyed the pricing chapter that dives deep into the thought process of pricing photography services and products as well as setting up bookkeeping organization and how that plays a role in everything.*"—**Amy Northard, The Accountants for Creatives®, https://amynorthardcpa.com**

"*From the very first page, Martinez and Maryanovich captivate readers with an engaging writing style and genuine enthusiasm for the craft. They take a step-by-step approach, covering everything from photography fundamentals and setting up your photography business to marketing strategies and client experience. Each chapter is filled with practical advice and real-world examples, making it easy for readers to apply the concepts to their own ventures.* Photography Business Basics *is a must-read for anyone aspiring to turn their passion for photography into a successful business. Martinez and Maryanovich's expertise shines through in every page, offering invaluable advice and inspiration. Whether you're just starting out or looking to take your photography business to the next level, this book is a game-changer. Don't miss out on the opportunity to learn from one of the industry's finest teams. Grab a copy today and watch your photography dreams soar."*—**Matthew Belter, CEO Bear Ice Company, Rockstar Photographer, www.iceboxphoto.com/about**

"Thoughts: LOVED THIS BOOK. Easy to read and a FABULOUS layout for how to get a real photo business accomplished. Smart, smart, smart. I found things I had not paid attention to when I ran a photo business eons ago, and loved the section about marketing, especially for today's market/younger photographers. While many of the inspirational messages in your book are ones I use in class, I think just having the basics—'how to figure this stuff out'—is CRITICAL to success. Most of the time I hear from the student artists that I work with in my department that this is all too overwhelming, that they haven't found a way to navigate this path—Then there is this book! HURRAY!!

I don't think you have to be a photographer to use this, as it could work in any creative artist's plan to have their own business and to plan for success. I am sending this link to some of my former students as well, and am also going to share it with our entrepreneurship program chairperson. We have many creatives and students that sit just outside of the 'business' department that need to know how creative people think, how we DON'T THINK but SHOULD THINK, and how we need to have a game plan to move forward. I am so thankful you all are on this and I wish you the very best with this endeavor."—**Benita VanWinkle, Associate Professor of Art | School of Arts and Design, High Point University North Carolina, www.highpoint.edu/faculty-staff/art-design/benita-vanwinkle**

*"*Photography Business Basics *is a well-written, timely, comprehensive book positively full of simple, intentional, and well-documented tips that will take you to the top of your craft fast. Natasha and Mark emphasize that your skill*

as a businessperson is the key, even more than your technical skills. They know what they're talking about and have chosen to generously share their passion and dedication to benefit you and your photography business. Just the two lists of Photography niches and Conversion methods alone, complete with multiple examples, will leave you thoughtful and inspired! Photography Business Basics *is the book you will wish you had when you started your photography business. So, don't delay—read it today."*—**Dr. Miluna Fausch, Pitch Perfect Soul Coach to Performers & Professionals, American Book Fest Business Books Finalist, Forbes Author, https://milunafauschmedia.com**

"I think it is a good fit for two of our classes. I really like your reverse engineering approach to the whole process. The book is easy to read and understand, with great real-world examples (Nikki Nash, Liz Harlin, ChangingMinds). I also like your CODB explanations …

And, you quoted one of my favorite movies, inconceivable …

I think this will be a great resource for students to leave the program with, so will either find a way to provide one to them or make it required reading. Thanks again for sharing your knowledge and experience!"—**David Mager, Chair of the Photography Department, New York Film Academy, www.nyfa.edu**

Preface

Congratulations and Welcome to *Photography Business Basics: A Professional Photographer's Guide to Financial Success*!

By picking up this book, you recognize that beginning, building, and maintaining a career as a Photographer requires business skill and sense.

The knowledge within these pages was acquired over a decade spent scouring the Internet and absorbing literally thousands of blog posts, webinars, and courses, then distilled to the essential techniques necessary to succeed.

As two real-world photography business entrepreneurs who've struggled and learned how to go from starving artists to savvy businesspersons, we hope to help the most number of people have the greatest success in photography by avoiding the pitfalls many artists in the business world fall prey to.

We truly hope the information in these chapters will help you.

Now, let's begin with the Basics ...

Introduction

So, you got into photography, maybe as a way to express your creativity as an artist. Capturing Images involves so many aspects: it's an art, it's a science, it's a feeling, it's technical. And these aspects are just the preliminaries.

Talent and skill with a camera is the starting point on the journey to becoming a professional Photographer, and this book is not about how to take better pictures. It's about becoming a better businessperson so that you can make a living taking pictures.

This book is also not about how to land a Photographer's agent. Landing an agent as a Photographer is akin to landing an agent as a model, or landing a minor or major league sports agent. It is an exceptional feat to accomplish, and if you are able to accomplish it, huge congratulations are in order.

Even with an agent on board, it is still important to become familiar with the contents in this book, as your rep will most likely not tell you what your 10-year plan and exit strategy are, how you should craft your Client experience, or how to manage your money. Finally, no one will or should care as much about your career than you, especially one who is only earning 15 to 20 percent of your income.

Here, we're going to assume you have the artistic ability and knowledge to take outstanding photos with every frame you capture. Now it's time to hone your business acumen.

The term "starving artist" stems from the long-held notion that creative people lack business sense. While this might be true in many cases, just as you learned about photography, you can learn about business too.

The good news is: The fundamentals of business hold true for any industry and rarely change dramatically.

If you can reprogram your mindset (more on this in Chapter 3) to recognize that you can apply your natural creative abilities to the business side of things (especially the marketing side), then this learning curve will definitely be more enjoyable for you.

Take it from Andy Warhol, one of the most famous and successful artists in history:

> *Being good in business is the most fascinating kind of art. Making money is art and working is art and good business is the best art.*[i]

CHAPTER 1

Photography Fundamentals

Now, before we embark on learning how to be good in business, we've included some advice on the creative side of photography, just for good measure, and hope you might find this helpful:

- Mark's general advice to all new Photographers includes studying with a professional Photographer in order to gain technical skills, and knowledge pertaining to how to deal with Clients and maintain the business side of your career.
- Analyzing the work and careers of successful Photographers in your field in order to gain inspiration and information on the business moves they made to get where they are in their careers is also a good thing to do.
- Passion and vision are key ingredients to success. Find out what you like about your photos, what kind and style of photos you are passionate about taking, and focus strongly on those areas. Make sure you believe in what you are doing. This will give you the confidence to assert your vision when working with Clients. This will also sustain you during the times when you feel overwhelmed or discouraged (it happens).
- When working with an assistant, remember that technical knowledge can be taught, while Client-savvy skills and going above-and-beyond in terms of what is expected of them are more useful skills. An assistant who will not offend Clients, is willing to work hard, and takes initiative are the most important qualifications.
- As far as cameras go, author Michael Baron said it best: *It's not the instrument that makes the music beautiful—it's the musician.*[ii] With everyone carrying a pro-level camera around in their pockets these days, it really comes down to the vision

you have for your photos, rather than the equipment you are using. Having written that, lenses are extremely important.

- Always set aside time to work on your craft, no matter how long you've been photographing for. There's always room for improvement, and the better you get, the better your business will get, because a good product can often sell itself ☺.

10 Elements of Professional Images

By Award-Winning Photographer
Mark Maryanovich

Mark Maryanovich has been invited to review portfolios for our students. We sought Mr. Maryanovich's expertise because he enjoys an elevated reputation as a photographer of tremendous skill and ability. We found that his real world experience as a successful and highly sought after photographer provided our students with a rare opportunity to learn from a master artist. We appreciate Mr. Maryanovich's invaluable service.

—Dick van Damme, Managing Director
The Photography Institute Pty. Ltd.

Some quick tips Mark compiled after conducting portfolio reviews for The Photography Institute, and the VanArts Media Arts School for Photography. Again, we hope you might find these helpful:

1. Always make sure the clothes are washed and wrinkle free before the Session.

2. Attention to details (such as the absence of small distracting specs, and whitened eyes of the subjects) adds strength to an Image.

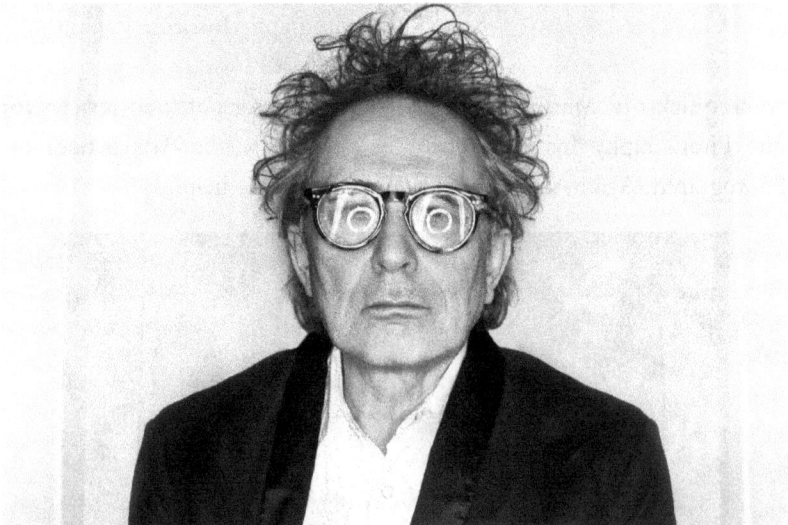

3. Use of an eye light is extremely important to ensure that the subject's eyes are the most prominent aspect of the photo.

4. Skin tones should be even.

5. Colors, highlights, reflections, and contrast can make a photo pop, and it's captivating when black-and-white tones work with the subject matter and mood you're aiming to achieve.

6. Horizon lines should be level.

7. Composition is everything.
    7.1. Cropping really helps.

8. Use a unique perspective. The ability to find interesting angles to create striking Images is easier these days, with cameras getting smaller and smaller.

9. A subject who is thinking loud always makes for a great photo.

10. Know where the Image will be used in order to place the subject during the shoot (e.g., if shooting for a magazine cover, leave lots of room at the top and along the sides for text; if shooting for Instagram, compose for a square or 4:5 aspect ratio; a social media banner Image lends itself to panoramic photos, and so on).

As in life, there's an EXCEPTION to every rule,
so BREAK them all and see where that gets you,
sometimes, ya never know …
It's been said, a PHOTO a day keeps the doctor AWAY.—MM

CHAPTER 2

Begin with the End

(The second of *The 7 Habits of Highly Effective People* by Stephen R. Covey,[iii] and the first book of our recommended reading, enjoy.)

Before you begin with the end, we feel that it's important to start with Market Proof.

Ask yourself, who do you want to be:

The food lover dreaming of turning his passion for cooking and hospitality into a living, who takes out a multi-zero loan; buys a space, furnishings, kitchen equipment and supplies; hires staff; and promotes a grand opening only to discover that no one is interested in spaghetti ice cream?

Or would you rather be the passionate food lover who makes small batches of spaghetti ice cream in the kitchen of his one-bedroom apartment, stands outside a toy store (with the proper permits and permission of course), offers his creations to folks as they enter and exit the establishment, and then asks if they might pay for a cone of pasta, and if so, how much would they pay?

Then, armed with this knowledge, he delves into the work of learning and implementing the business basics as outlined in this book, investing in the restaurant space, furnishings, equipment, supplies, and staff, knowing that he has a sellable product and an educated estimate of how much he can expect to earn.

The second example is maybe the less exciting or glamorous route, though it's also the route that will lead away from financial ruin and existential despair.

So, as a Photographer, we suggest, before investing in that huge studio space, the newest, latest and greatest equipment, software, and so on, take the camera you currently own or have access to (even if it's your smartphone), photograph some people (ideally in the genre you hope to focus on and ideally with people other than your family and friends), and ask them if they would pay for your services, and if so, how much.

We were going to put this analogy in under the chapter on Pricing, as we truly feel that even if your first market tests do not go well, when you are truly driven, and you truly want to become a Photographer with a successful, sustainable business, you will work until you:

a. Improve your product
b. Find the folks willing to pay you for your work, or
c. Do both

After all, spaghetti ice cream is apparently a popular dish.

If, however, you get discouraged, and figure out that this whole professional photography idea really isn't up your alley, it's better to find out now that you are no longer interested, before reading and then implementing all of the suggestions that follow.

If you've done your Market Testing and you're still a gamer, let's begin ...

As you begin to build your photography business, the best place to start is at the end.

Having a crystal-clear vision in mind of what you would like to have achieved allows you to reverse engineer the steps to get there.

Picture yourself 10 years from now and write down what you see. You can do this in a notebook, and add photos of key elements, such as the city you see yourself living in, the place you call home, possibly the car you drive, your family and loved ones that are an important part of your life, now and in the future.

Include things such as how old you are, your dominant feelings (happy, fulfilled, content), and a paragraph or page of what a day in your life is like at that time.

Also, be specific on what your biggest accomplishments are.

It's fun to get creative here and remove any constraints or limits on what you're imagining. As the saying goes:

Shoot for the moon. Even if you miss, you'll land among the stars.
—Norman Vincent Peale[iv]

One other aspect to think about during this exercise is your exit strategy, even if this might be beyond 10 years from now. Maybe you see yourself working well into your 90s, or maybe you see yourself retiring one day. If you do plan to retire, write down when that day is and what that looks like.

Retirement for a business owner is different from someone retiring from a job. For more traditional businesses, exit strategies can include being bought out by a larger company, going public, franchising, or product licensing.

If you plan to be the sole Photographer in your business, then franchising or turning your company over to another owner might not make a lot of sense. If you'd like to see this business you're going to build live on long after you retire, then this will mean a different strategy in designing and building it, aspects we'll work on in the following chapters.

Right now, the point is to visualize your future in detail, including your exit plan.

Having written that, here's a story to keep in mind about a Mexican Fisherman and an Investment Banker written by Heinrich Böll[v]:

An American Investment Banker was at the pier of a small coastal Mexican village when a small boat with just one fisherman docked. Inside the small boat were several large yellowfin tuna. The American complimented the Mexican on the quality of his fish and asked how long it took to catch them.

The Mexican replied, "Only a little while." The American then asked why didn't he stay out longer and catch more fish? The Mexican said he had enough to support his family's immediate needs. The American then asked, "But what do you do with the rest of your time?"

The Mexican fisherman said, "I sleep late, fish a little, play with my children, take siestas with my wife, Maria, stroll into the village each evening where I sip wine, and play guitar with my amigos. I have a full and busy life."

The American scoffed, "I am a Harvard MBA and could help you. You should spend more time fishing and with the proceeds, buy a bigger boat. With the proceeds from the bigger boat, you could buy several boats, eventually you would have a fleet of fishing boats. Instead of selling your catch to a middleman you would sell directly to the processor, eventually opening your own cannery. You would control the product, processing, and distribution.

You would need to leave this small coastal fishing village and move to Mexico City, then LA, and eventually New York City, where you will run your expanding enterprise."

The Mexican fisherman asked, "But, how long will this all take?"

To which the American replied, "15–20 years."

"But what then?" asked the Mexican.

The American laughed and said, "That's the best part. When the time is right you would announce an IPO and sell your company stock to the public and become very rich, you would make millions!"

"Millions—then what?"

The American said, "Then you would retire. Move to a small coastal fishing village where you would sleep late, fish a little, play with your kids, take siestas with your wife, stroll to the village in the evenings where you could sip wine and play your guitar with your amigos."

Building a business takes time. Running a business will consume your life for the first 3 to 5 to 7 to 10 years, demanding all of your abilities and attention at many junctures. It will sometimes dishearten you, humble you, and exhaust you. It will also, when things work out, give you a sense of fulfillment and an incredibly rewarding feeling in a way that no job can match.

Life is short, and once you hit 40, it moves exponentially quicker.

The key here is: before you begin building, ask yourself what you really want, now, in the future, and on your way to the future. Life is what you make it.

CHAPTER 3

Mindset

Watch your thoughts, they become words;
watch your words, they become actions;
watch your actions, they become habits;
watch your habits, they become character;
watch your character, for it becomes your destiny.

—Often attributed to Frank Outlaw,
Late president of the Bi-Lo Stores[vi]

We get it. You became a Photographer because you wanted to be an artist not a businessperson. If you were interested in business, you would have gone into business, right?

Well, if you'd like to earn money as a Photographer, then there's no escaping becoming a businessperson. The very definition of business according to Wikipedia is:

"(T)he practice of making one's living or making money by producing or buying and selling products. It is also 'any activity or enterprise entered into for profit.'"[vii]

Now, as an artist, the upcoming chapters may seem like trigonometry, calculus, or Latin. So it's important to approach them with a beginner's mind. Erase any prejudices you might have, or any limiting beliefs that you can't or won't understand what's ahead.

It's also important to realize that a lot of this information might sit on the surface of your understanding for days, weeks, months, or even years before it actually sinks in and becomes practical working knowledge. Understand without judgment that this is neither here nor there, it simply is.

Once empty and ready to learn, one lesson to firmly plant inside your mind is that you cannot get emotional when it comes to your business.

It is vital to set emotions aside in many business situations such as:

- Dealing with unhappy Clients (though ideally with the lessons you learn in Chapter 7, unhappy Clients will be a rarity and ultimately nonexistent)
- Experiencing failure: a marketing plan that does not go as hoped for (it happens), a time of drought in sales, and so on

Again, understand without judgment that this is neither here nor there, these things just happen.

Most crucially, your emotions cannot dictate your actions on a daily basis when building and running your business. If you work on your business only when you feel like it, and you don't work on your business when you don't feel like it, then your chances for advancement, achievement, and success will be slim.

Both Denzel and Oprah have said it:

(D)o what you got to do now, so you can do what you want to do later[viii]

—Denzel Washington

Do what you have to do until you can do what you want to do.[ix]

—Oprah Winfrey

The "what" that you want to do later is what you picture in your 10-year plan, after your exit strategy (while keeping the Mexican Fisherman in mind). Do what you have to do each and every day in order to get there.

A motto to keep in mind while on this journey is that these are all tasks that you *GET* to do, not *HAVE* to do. This subtle shift in words means a lot. Consider that a large percentage of the world is fighting for basic needs like food, clothing, shelter, and freedom, and you get to spend your time creating the business of your dreams.

An attitude of gratitude and realization of how truly blessed we are should be enough to keep us going. However, building a business takes time. You may work for months and years on creating your marketing plan, honing your sales, creating and implementing your systems, and it might seem like nothing is happening, that is, no Clients, no sales, no progress.

Like the tiny acorn planted, after a period of dormancy, in four to five years, the seedling will gradually grow and transform into a sapling tree. Then years and decades later, this one little acorn seed turns into a full-grown oak.[x]

Being human, there will be plenty of times when you will feel like blowing everything off, especially when the fruits of your labor aren't apparent. This is where willpower comes in.

Figure out how you can best motivate yourself. It might be taking those images from the notebook of your 10-year plan and hanging them in plain sight above your bed or over your TV, so you have to literally move them before you can start watching your favorite shows, placing sticky notes with motivational sayings strategically throughout your home, or creating a playlist of songs that amplify your energy.

Whatever it is, do it now and settle in for the long haul. This is a marathon, not a sprint.

CHAPTER 4

Reverse Engineering

With your 10-year plan now in place, it's time to work backward to get there.

Your life after your exit strategy is Point B. Where you are now is Point A. So let's begin with exactly where you are now.

While this may seem like a disconnect, we're going to start with your current financial situation, not branding, not sales, not marketing; we're going to start with your daily spending habits.

People go into business to make money. And money will determine a large part of your business plan in terms of how much you would like to earn and how much you're able to spend (or invest) in order to earn more money.

Again, mindset is key here. However you feel about money, earning it and spending it, it's now time to become friends with it and embrace its power to make things happen.

As actor Steve Harvey said:

Money allows you to become more of who you really are ... If you are a generous person, more money will allow you to be more generous. If you're a sharer, you're going to be more sharing.[xi]

If money wasn't a concern, you would buy the exact clothes, car, home, and furnishings that you truly want. You would express yourself best through these purchases. How we spend our money shows what we value most, and that's what makes money valuable.

Money is rarely the end goal in and of itself, it is the conduit that enables us to experience the end goal.

With a healthy relationship with money in place, building your business will be much more enjoyable and perhaps easier than if the concept of money makes you uncomfortable. We'll even go so far as to say that an unwillingness to overcome this discomfort is a nonstarter to starting a business. You might be better off if you forget the whole thing and get a job or find another way to spend your life.

Like any skill, money management can be learned. It requires discipline and determination to master. If you need help getting acquainted with money, we highly recommend reading *Think and Grow Rich* by Napoleon Hill. This book is a goldmine of wisdom pertaining to money, business, and life in general. Enjoy.

Ready to start the reverse engineering process?

Okay great! Let's go:

Your Spending Log

This is exactly what it sounds like: a log of your spending.

For the next 30 days, write down in a notebook (it can be the same notebook as your 10-year plan, it's up to you) or a spreadsheet (a spreadsheet may be easier) absolutely everything you spend money on every day. (If you would like a copy of our Spending Log Template in Google Sheets or Excel format, please e-mail us at: natasha@markmaryanovich .com with the subject line Templates, and we'll be happy to send one along!)

This is a great place to mention that now is the time to get into the habit of getting a receipt for everything. And we mean everything. That $0.23 banana you bought at Trader Joe's? Get a receipt for it, especially if you paid cash, and don't feel silly about asking for it.

Yes, sometimes you won't be able to get a receipt, and if this is the case, then write down what you spent on a slip of paper with the date and payment method (cash, debit, credit card, and so on). All of these receipts you collect will go into an easily accessible envelope.

Your Spending Log should have the following headings:

Table 4.1 Spending Log

			Payment Method (as applicable to you):					
Date	Description: Where did you spend this money?	What exactly did you buy?	Cash	Debit	Credit card	Sales tax	Subtotal (price before sales tax)	Total (exactly how much you paid including sales tax)
Month/ Day/ Year	Trader Joe's	One banana	$0.23			$0.00	$0.23	$0.23

Do this for every single purchase you make, every single day.

We recommend continuing this process for more than 30 days, maybe even until you reach your exit strategy point, though at the end of the 30 days, you'll have a good idea of where you spend your money, and what you value most. If your spending is out of line with your values, you can start making changes. This process makes you aware of this misalignment.

You can now also identify spending leaks and start plugging them. You'll see, for example, that the $2.50 convenience charge for using the ATM by your home, plus the charge from your bank for using the out-of-network ATM quickly add up when used even a couple times each month throughout the year.

You can eliminate this expense by planning ahead and going to an ATM that won't charge you, or by getting cash back when buying groceries or at the post office for no charge as well. Now by planning ahead that $2.50+ can be spent in a way that you truly value without sacrificing the convenience it was paying for. (Side note, do people still use ATMs a couple of times a month? At any rate, we hope you still get the point.)

After you've logged your spending for 30 days, it's time to ask yourself:

- What are three ways I can increase my income?
- What are five ways I could reduce spending?

This is where your creativity comes in, and these ideas and answers will be specific to you. Here are some examples if you're drawing a blank:

Ways to increase your income could include:

Idea #1:   Diversify your product offering (more on this in the next chapter)

Idea #2:   Charge more money for your services (more on this in the next chapter)

Idea #3:   Use a cash back debit/credit card

Ways to reduce spending could include:

Idea #1:   Dine out less

Idea #2:   Pay off a credit card or anything charging interest

Idea #3:   Reduce your COGS and O&GE: Shop around and wait to buy things when they are on sale, especially big-ticket items (more on this in the next chapter)

Idea #4:   Buy subscriptions at the annual fee (it's usually cheaper than paying monthly)

Idea #5:   Eliminate ATM withdrawal fees ☺

Write down next to each idea how much you estimate it will add to your income and how much it will reduce your spending (thereby adding to your income).

If you need help managing your money, we recommend reading Dave Ramsey's *The Total Money Makeover*. While some people disagree with his stance on credit (and we used a credit card in Idea #3 as a way to increase your income) his approach to money is simple, and easy to both understand and implement. Enjoy.

Taking out the emotion is important to this process as well. Don't judge yourself too harshly or too lightly: just look at the numbers and if you need to, begin to adjust your spending actions so that they align with your values.

CHAPTER 5

Pricing

Now that we have our 30-day Spending Log in place, let's continue along our seemingly backward path to building our business.

It's time to look at our pricing.

Pricing? You might think, and a myriad of statements come to mind: I don't even know what I'm selling yet; I don't know how to sell; I don't know who I'm selling to, ….

The response to all of those statements stems from pricing and reverse engineering.

Pricing is both art and mathematics, and it may take weeks, months, or even years to get it right. So it's important to have a formula to work with from the outset.

Again, let's begin with the end in mind. Regardless of how much you're currently earning from photography (e.g., $0/year or $50,000/year), think about exactly how much you would like to earn in the year ahead. Write this number down.

Now, let's go back to your Spending Log and look at your expenses.

Expenses for a business owner fall into three categories:

1. Personal:
   Examples include groceries, clothing, entertainment, and such.
2. COGS: Cost Of Goods Sold
   COGS are expenses that you incurred because you needed to buy an Item specifically for a Photoshoot. Examples include location fees, props for a specific shoot and that shoot only, travel to the shoot, merchant credit card fees (PayPal/Venmo/Stripe Fees) on payments from specific shoots, and so on.

   If you have no Photoshoots and therefore no sales, you will not have any COGS.

3. O&GE: Overhead and General Expenses

O&GE are expenses that you incur whether or not you have any sales. These include your website and marketing materials (more on this later), insurance, office/studio rent and utilities, taxes, and so on.

If you are just starting out, you may not have any COGS or O&GE to look at. Or perhaps you already are in business and have these numbers to reference. Either way, the Professional Photographers of America (PPA)'s benchmark recommendations are:

COGS:	25 percent of your sales
O&GE:	35 percent of your sales
Total COGS + O&GE:	60 percent of your sales

Before we go any further, now seems like a great place to mention how highly we recommend becoming a member of the PPA. A lot of our knowledge we learned from the PPA's extensive webisode series on the business of photography. Also, membership includes being listed in their Find A Photographer website (great for marketing) and certain types of insurance: www.ppa.com.

We'd also like to mention that this information is not a substitute for engaging a qualified accountant and/or a bookkeeper.

And once you hire a qualified accountant and/or bookkeeper it is still worthwhile to know, understand, and keep on top of your income and expenses, because, after all, it is your money, and your sales and expenditures are a great barometer for your business.

Also, by keeping track of your sales and spending in an organized fashion, your accountant and/or bookkeeper will love you for it, and you may be able to reduce this expense (see Chapter 4) as you will reduce the time they need to spend on logging your income and categorizing your expenses.

From here, we're going to presuppose you've had some sales and incurred some COGS and O&GE. We've included some suggested categories to include in a spreadsheet of your own.

Each category can have the same headings as your Spending Log, and you might want to keep these categories on a different sheet within the same spreadsheet of your Spending Log, so that you can easily copy and paste each expenditure into its appropriate category after you've logged it.

We like to group these categories by month, that is, your COGS spreadsheet will have the categories listed vertically under January, then listed vertically again under February, and so on. We do the same for the O&GE categories, and for the Personal expense categories on different sheets. This enables you to look at your spending each month.

Again, please consult with a qualified accountant and/or bookkeeper regarding the current specifications of what can be deducted and how much can be deducted as legitimate business expenses. The point here is to just keep track of your expenses in the categories so you can adjust toward the benchmarks as necessary.

Your accountant and/or bookkeeper will most likely encourage you to use a financial software system such as QuickBooks. In the beginning, we think it's important to be incredibly specific on tracking and categorizing each and every expense, and doing this manually using a spreadsheet allows this to happen.

COGS Categories:

Accessories/Packaging
Contract Labor: production and assistant labor
Editing, Retouching, Album Design, and so on
Frame and Album Expense
Lab and Printing Expense
Location Rentals
Meals Related to shoot
Merchant Credit Card Fees: online sales transaction fees
Music Licensing Fees
Photographic Supplies: items related to a specific job
Production Employee Payroll
Production Employee Payroll Taxes
Props/Accessories: only those related to a specific Photoshoot
Sales Commissions
Shipping Costs: Client-related

Travel for Specific Client Work:
    Airfare
    Lodging
    Transportation

When it comes to COGS, it's important at this point for you to think through how you will be delivering your Images to your Clients.

Will you be delivering on a thumb drive or as finished, framed prints? If so, include this as a COGS.

If you plan to only deliver digital Images (and you may be leaving money on the table if you are—more on this later), then this depends on your Gallery delivery system (more on this also later). If your Gallery delivery system comes with your website hosting platform or studio management software, then this could fall under your O&GE Marketing Expense. If it is a thumb drive you deliver, then this is a COGS expense under Accessories/Packaging.

Again, your bookkeeper/accountant will know best. The idea here is to have the expense logged, somewhere in your master spreadsheet.

O&GE Categories:

    Overhead
        Insurance
        Maintenance
        Property Tax
        Rent
        Storage
        Utilities
    Administrative
        Accounting
        Auto: Car Rentals/Insurance/Repairs
        Auto: Fuel
        Auto: Mileage Reimbursements
        Education Dues, Memberships, and Subscriptions
        Interest and Exchange Rate

Legal

Office: Computer Expenses (including computer equipment under $500), software fees, office supplies, office meals

Postage: not related to a specific Client

Professional Fees

Props/Accessories: not related to one specific Photoshoot

Taxes and Licenses

Telephone

General Expenses

Marketing:

Advertising

Display Rental/Expense

Donations

Entertainment

Marketing: General

Parking

Postage: Promotions

Printing: Promotions

Promotions: Events

Referrals

Taxis

Website/Hosting Expenses

Employee Expense

Owner's Compensation

Capital Expenditures

Items over $500: computers/cameras/lenses/and so on.

You should treat this as a bill, and set aside (save) money for upgrading your equipment, computer, phone every 2 to 5 years.

Personal Expense Categories:

ATM withdrawal fees

Cards and gifts for family and friends

Clothing

Entertainment

General: any personal expense that doesn't fall into any of the other
  categories

Giving: the dollar you gave to a homeless person, the couple bucks
  you put in the Salvation Army kettle, and so on

Groceries

Grooming

Household

Meals out

Medical

Postage: mailing cards and items to your family and friends

While you might not have expenses for every category right now, it's a good idea to list them in case you need them in the future.

And those receipts including the ones for all the single bananas you bought at Trader Joe's throughout the month that are currently living in one envelope? At the end of the month those receipts are photographed with your phone or scanned by your accounting software and then uploaded to your cloud or computer hard drive (some people like to photograph their receipts daily, and this is a good idea, as sometimes receipt ink tends to fade even within a month).

These digital and hard copies are then transferred: digital receipts go into different folders on your desktop, while paper receipts go into different envelopes. These folders and envelopes are ones you created and labeled with the name of each category. For example,

An envelope/folder called "COGS"
An envelope/folder called "O&GE"
An envelope/folder called "Personal Expenses"

So now ideally you have your envelopes/folders, master spreadsheet with your COGS, O&GE and Personal Expense sheets, and the expenses you logged for the past 30 days entered into their appropriate categories. Bonus points if you've created the categories for the months ahead, ready and waiting to be filled in with your upcoming expenses.

Now tally up your sales, COGS and O&GE, do the math and see if they fall into the PPA Benchmarks of:

25 percent for COGS
35 percent for O&GE

If not, it's time to adjust by asking yourself the same question from Chapter 4:

• What are five ways I can reduce spending?

After you've come up with your five answers, add your total COGS and O&GE and subtract this number from the amount you would like to earn in the year ahead.

To keep things simple, let's say the amount you'd like to earn annually is $100,000.

This is an ambitious goal, though it can most certainly be done. This leads nicely to another resource we highly recommend:

Charles Lewis Photography:
https://cjlewis.com/home-page.html

Charles and his team provide valuable tips on how to earn $100,000 annually as a Photographer. While his techniques might not be applicable to your own photography business style, the principles he teaches are extremely helpful to know.

According to Salary.com, the average freelance Photographer salary in the United States is $77,585 as of December 1, 2024. This salary "can go up to $101,102 or down to $59,637, but most earn between $68,191 and $89,895."[xii] Whether this is gross or net is unclear.

Getting back to the basics, gross income means your total sales before any expenses (COGS and O&GE) while net means your income after your COGS and O&GE have been subtracted.

When you thought about exactly how much you would like to earn in the year ahead at the beginning of this chapter (we're going with $100,000 for simplicity's sake), this would be your gross income.

Now that we've subtracted our 60 percent for COGS and O&GE, we're left with $40,000, your net income. From this $40,000, you will eventually be allocating an amount for your time and labor. This is your Photographer's salary, and technically, you'll use your Photographer's salary and Photographer's salary alone to pay for your personal expenses.

The amount left over after deducting your Photographer's salary will be used for building your retirement nest egg, emergency, contingency and sinking funds (see Dave Ramsey's *The Total Money Makeover*), and potentially, bonuses.

If $40,000 annually in net profit works for you in terms of your personal expenses, various funds, and saving for after your exit strategy, then great! We can proceed.

If not, adjust your gross income number to more than $100,000 and do the math again, subtracting your COGS and O&GE (that are ideally at the benchmark percentages).

Once you have a net income figure that you're happy with, it's time to ask yourself the next question:

How many Photoshoots would you ideally like to be paid to do each week, which adds up to each month, and subsequently each year?

Before you answer this question, let's factor in your time.

It's a good idea to type this out in a document you can save, as it will serve as the basis for part of your systems that we'll get to in Chapter 10.

List all the steps you perform to fulfill a Photoshoot, along with the time each step takes. For example, a 1-hour Photography Session might be stepped out as follows:

Client research:	1 hour
Pre-Photoshoot consultation with Client:	45 minutes
Contracting and invoicing your Client:	30 minutes
Location research/studio booking:	45 minutes
Actual Photography Session:	1 hour
Total travel time to and from Photoshoot:	1 hour
Importing, backing up, editing, and Gallery upload time:	2 hours
In-Person Sales/order fulfillment:	2 hours
Total Hours:	9 hours

It's important to keep in mind here that we are not including the time you'll be spending on marketing, sales, administration, business planning, and so on. This is strictly the hours you spend actually being a Photographer.

Conservatively, it's safe to say that as a business owner, you should be spending 10 to 20 hours a week on business planning, marketing, sales, and administration for a total of 40 to 80 hours each month or 480 to 960 hours each year.

It's also helpful to keep in mind that the average employee works 50 hours each week or 200 hours each month and 2,400 hours each year.

Now let's return to the question: How many Photoshoots would you ideally like to be paid to do each week, which adds up to each month, and subsequently each year?

Divide your ideal gross income figure by this number of Photoshoots. Let's say you'd like to do:

- One Photoshoot per week/work 9 hours per week as a Photographer
  This equals:
- Four Photoshoots per month/working 36 hours per month as a Photographer
  This equals:
- 48 Photoshoots per year/working 432 hours per year as a Photographer
  $100,000 per year/48 = $2,083.33

This means you would have to charge $2,083.33 per Photoshoot.

If you'd like to shoot four times per week, or 16 times per month, or 192 times per year, then the math looks like this:

- Four Photoshoots per week/working 36 hours per week as a Photographer
  This equals:
- 16 Photoshoots per month/working 144 hours per month as a Photographer

This equals:
- 192 Photoshoots per year/working 1,728 hours per year as a Photographer
  $100,000 per year/192 = $520.83

This means you would have to charge $520.83 per Photoshoot.

Yes, this is a big difference, and yes, most likely you will be offering longer or shorter shoots, different packages, and different products at different price points (as you should). And also yes, many times you may be working at discounted rates just to keep the sales coming in.

The point being here is to have a benchmark based on your expenses that serves as the starting point for the packages and products you will offer, along with their prices. This benchmark also begins to delineate the type of Client you will be serving and the products and services you will need to provide to maintain this benchmark.

Having these benchmark prices also lets your Client know when they are getting a deal, and you should let them know that (more on this later).

Also importantly, you are looking at your time. Again, we are not including the time you'll be spending on marketing, sales, administration, business planning, and so on. These are strictly the hours you spend actually being a Photographer. To figure out your Photographer's salary, you want to establish an hourly rate for yourself, one that takes into account the current minimum wage along with your skill and experience.

Arbitrarily and to keep things simple, let's set your pay rate at $20 per hour.

At $20 per hour, you would earn $180 for your labor involved in one 1-hour Photoshoot that involves 9 hours of your time and labor.

At one 1-hour Photoshoot per week, your Photographer's annual salary would be:

$$48 \times \$180 = \$8,640$$

At four 1-hour Photoshoots per week, your Photographer's annual salary would be:

$$192 \times \$180 = \$34,560$$

Again, a big difference. And you might be asking, what does this matter, how much my salary as a Photographer is, isn't everything that's left over after subtracting my COGS and O&GE just going to be mine anyways?

The answer is, technically, yes.

Though there are at least a couple of different reasons why you should take the time to figure this out.

The first reason is that if your exit strategy includes hiring a Photographer to replace you, or selling your business to another entity, it's essential to know how much the Photographer's salary is.

The second reason is if you forget to include compensating yourself for your time, your pricing may include only the costs needed to cover your expenses, with not much or nothing left over for you to pay for things like food and clothing.

Third, the money you get to pay yourself will keep you motivated as you work extremely hard on building and growing your business.

The importance of establishing your Photographer's salary becomes even more clear as we now learn and implement a strategy for managing your cash flow.

Put simply, cash flow

refers to payments made into or out of a business. ... It can also refer more specifically to a real or virtual movement of money. Cash flow, in its narrow sense, is a payment (in a currency), especially from one central bank account to another. The term "cash flow" is mostly used to describe payments that are expected to happen in the future, are thus uncertain, and therefore need to be forecast with cash flows.[xiii]

It's good practice to receive payment for your Photoshoot by splitting the total amount into an advance and balance. The advance can be as little or as much as you like (say, 20 to 50 percent) that's due as soon as you confirm the shoot date with your Client, to hold that day and time for them. (Refunds and cancellations will be discussed in Chapter 7.)

The balance should be due once their Images are ready to be delivered and you should require payment of the balance before you deliver your work (more on this also in Chapter 7).

The reason to split the total payment up is twofold:

One, it makes for better cash flow as money does tend to get spent as soon as you have it, and splitting it up enables you to budget better.

Two, it takes the pressure off you and the Client as it seems to beget higher expectations if payment is paid in full before the Photoshoot. Also, if something happens and you do have to refund the Client's money, 20 to 50 percent will be easier for you to manage than the full 100 percent.

Ideally, you're using a studio management software (covered in Chapter 9) that keeps a record of all of your invoices, money received, and money due.

Even still, it's also a good idea to keep a running budget of your own, a separate sheet within your Spending Log, COGS and O&GE spreadsheet that lists the money you have received and are expecting.

Also ideally, you have a business checking and savings account set up, and your bank offers a savings goal account feature (like Bank of America does). With this feature, you can set up different accounts within your savings account and give them different names.

You can then allocate specific amounts from your savings account into the sub-goal accounts. The money is still in your savings account and accessible, it's just been grouped into different categories, like so:

Income Account: your initial Savings Account
Within this account, you'll create:

1. Your COGS account
2. Your O&GE account
3. Your Tax account: where you'll reserve a percentage of money for taxes
4. Your Owner's Compensation account: this is where your Photographer's salary lives
5. Your Profit account: this is your celebration account: bonus money that does not go back into your business or get used for your personal expenses

Once you have these sub-accounts set up, each and every time you receive a payment (advance or balance), transfer the funds (if necessary) to your Income Account.

From there, transfer:

- 25 percent of the payment amount into your COGS account
- 35 percent of the payment amount into your O&GE account
- 15 percent of the payment amount into your Tax account
- 20 percent of the payment amount into your Owner's Compensation account
- 5 percent of the payment amount into your Profit account

Then, pay for your COGS out of your COGS account, your O&GE bills out of your O&GE account, and your personal expenses out of your Owner's Compensation account.

Yes, there will be times when you need to transfer money from your Owner's Compensation account or Profit Account to cover your COGS or O&GE. And yes, 20 percent of your deposits may or may not cover the salary you worked out in the math formula above.

The point to having this system in place is that it lets you know how your business is doing and if your pricing is where you need it to be.

Don't touch the funds in your Tax account and use this money to pay your quarterly installments (as advised by your bookkeeper and/or accountant), and try not to touch the funds in your Profit account.

Saving money is an important discipline to start implementing as a behavioral pattern sooner rather than later. If you find you're unable to set aside 5 percent from each deposit, start with 1 percent and then add another 1 percent when you can, until you reach 5 percent.

Use this money for celebrations or to treat yourself at planned times with planned items. Or try to exercise self-discipline and watch this Profit sub-account grow. As Albert Einstein once said:

Compound interest is the eighth wonder of the world. He who under-stands it, earns it ... he who doesn't ... pays it.[xiv]

Once you become familiar with money, you'll learn that it's very psychological. Seeing your savings grow even at 1 percent increments creates a very pleasant feeling. Keeping money in a different account somehow stops you from wanting to spend it as you might do if it was just left floating in one master account.

There are endless theories on money management, and one of them is to pay yourself first. By allocating your 20 percent to your Owner's Compensation first, and then the 15 percent to your taxes, and then forcing yourself to make do with whatever's left over for COGS and O&GE will force you to rethink the amounts you're paying for your Photoshoot-related items, equipment, and bills.

Of course, you should never cut corners to sacrifice the quality of the products and services you deliver as that will eventually affect the amount of money coming in and the ultimate success of your business.

Now let's talk about budgeting.

Budgeting is an important skill for a business owner to master. It is much easier to budget if you know exactly how much money you will earn in each month, and as freelancers, this rarely happens.

Moreover, Photography tends to be a seasonal business. You'll have your busy months and less busy months, depending on the type of Images you offer.

This is where the percentage amounts for your sub-bank accounts come in handy:

If you receive a large Session fee, stick to the percentages, even if the COGS related to this particular Photoshoot do not tally up to 25, and 35 percent of this big paycheck exceeds your O&GE. By keeping that money in those sub-accounts, it will be there for the offseason.

While it's more difficult to budget on predictions, it's even more important to do so. Budget down to the last dollar you hope will come in for your COGS, O&GE, and personal expenses. You can create your monthly budgets on a separate sheet within your Spending Log, COGS and O&GE spreadsheet. A sample budget might look like this:

Table 5.1 Sample Budget

Income	Planned	Received	Total	Income Allocation	Outflow	Date Due	Budgeted Cost	Total	Actual Cost	Date Paid
List the name of the Client you're expecting payments from	List the dollar amount of the expected payment	List the dollar amount you actually received	Add up the total payments you received during the month	Profit account (5%) Owner's Comp. account (20%) Tax account (15%) COGS account (25%) O&GE account (35%) From the O&GE account: list the bills you will be paying From the COGS account: list the shoot expenses you will be paying	List all of your bills here	List the date the bill is due next to it	List the amount of the bill next to it	Add up all your monthly bills	List how much you paid for each bill (ideally the full amount)	List the date you paid each bill
					If you like, here you can set a budget for your monthly spend on food, clothing, entertainment, and list each amount you spend in these categories throughout the month.					
					If you do a continuous tally on your spending here, it will let you know if you are on track with your budget limits.					
					Personal Expense Monthly Total:					
					Owner's Compensation for this month:					
						Budget for month:	Amount Spent:	Date Spent:	Category Total:	
					Groceries:	Insert rows as applicable				
					Clothing:	Insert rows as applicable				
					Entertainment:	Insert rows as applicable				

It is worth mentioning here that you should learn and implement a system that works for you. Maybe you like using an adding machine or abacus (today, the stand-alone calculator that isn't also a phone), pen, pencil, or budgeting app. Use what you like and what you're most comfortable with so that the process is something you will enjoy more and maybe even look forward to.

(If you would like a copy of our Budget Template in Google Sheets or Excel format, please e-mail us at: natasha@markmaryanovich.com with the subject line Templates, and we'll be happy to send one along!)

While we're on the subject of budgeting, as a business owner the other skill you'll want to master is budgeting your time.

There are several apps, theories, and blog posts about time management. We find that an effective way to manage all the things you will *get* to do in terms of running your business is to set aside an hour or so every Friday or Saturday (just some time before the next week starts) and look at your week ahead and the tasks you *get* to accomplish.

In essence, plan your next week, not your next day. This will allow you to set aside blocks of time, say two hours every morning responding to e-mails and social media posts/comments, three hours every afternoon working on your marketing and sales, two hours each evening planning and thinking about where your business is going.

The point is if you schedule this way, you can remain flexible and shift things around as the week progresses and days get away from you (it happens). This is much more motivating than just transferring your leftover activities you didn't get to onto the next day's list and then the next day's, then the next day's, and so on.

Again, do this in an app, your Gmail calendar, a day timer, or printable loose-leaf paper that you hole punch and keep in a three-ring binder. Use whatever method is most appealing to you.

Alright. Now we have an idea of how much we'd like to charge and how often we'd like to shoot based on our expenses. Excellent. Now it's time to figure out exactly who we're going to charge to Photograph.

CHAPTER 6

Target Market Personas

Ideally, you now have an idea of how many times you would like to shoot per year, and, consequently, how much you will have to charge per Photoshoot.

This number provides the basis for the products and packages you will offer.

It's a well-known business theory that offering a multitude of product choices tends to overwhelm and confuse potential Clients, and a confused and overwhelmed mind shuts down when it comes to making decisions.

Three seems to be the magic number in product offerings (think: small, medium, large). The easier to understand what each product provides, the easier it is for your potential Client to decide on the product they want.

While you may not be able to limit your products and packages to just three, do try to keep the options limited. Ever been to In-N-Out Burger?[xv] Exactly. And there's always a line up around the block at each and every location.

Now, you have your basic number of what you will charge to work your desired amount of Sessions per year to earn your desired gross income. It's a good idea to make this number your Medium-sized price, because people tend to buy the item in the middle price range.

Next it's time to figure out your Small product offering. How much will you charge for this? Again, go back and do the math of how many hours it will take you (maybe this is a 15-minute mini-Session), and the bare minimum you can charge, given your fixed expenses of COGS and O&GE.

Then it's time to figure out your Large-sized price and how much you will charge for this by going back and doing the math again. Of course, your profit margin will be much larger here.

After you have your three price points figured out, it's time to start planning what each price point will include.

Your lowest price point should be your Minimum Viable Offer (MVO): the simplest product, service, or package you can deliver to your Clients while still providing value.

This brings us to our next highly recommend reading, Nikki Nash's *Market Your Genius*.[xvi] In her book, Nikki writes about the MVO, while succinctly and inspirationally outlining strategies to build your audience (of your Target Market Personas) and accomplish your business goals. She also provides worksheets, videos, and audio files for support as you implement her tools for success. Please read and enjoy!

Maybe your MVO is a quick, 15-minute Session, without any re-touched Images, definitely no prints, with a Gallery expiration date.

Your Medium package should then offer more than that and provide much more value to your Clients so it makes sense for them to spend more on that offering.

Your Large package should then offer more than your Medium package and provide even more value to your Clients so it makes sense for them to purchase this option.

We're figuring this out in broad strokes at this stage, as there are many more steps we *get* to go through to finalize (for now) your packages. What is important at this point is looking at the prices you plan to charge.

Going back to our sample math in Chapter 5, the Photographer who would like to work once a week might be thinking of charging like the below:

Package One: $1,200
Package Two: $2,085
Package Three: $3,250

These are arbitrary prices we've come up with here. The numbers you come up with should absolutely be based on the math of your COGS, O&GE, personal expenses, exit strategy specific to you, and then the products or services you will offer and the value you will provide.

The Photographer who would like to work four times each week might be thinking of charging as shown here:

Package One: $295
Package Two: $525
Package Three: $700

Again, these prices are arbitrary, and keep in mind that the Photographer who would like to work four times per week will most likely have the added expense of an administrative assistant, postproduction assistant, and so on, because they will be spending most of their time shooting.

The Photographer shooting once per week at a higher price point should factor in higher COGS for providing higher quality gifts and products Clients expect from a more expensive luxury brand.

It's worthwhile noting here that pricing is extremely psychological as well. After all, it has to do with money. There are many theories about setting prices that end in .99 or the number five or zero.

We feel that how you choose to set your prices reflects on your brand (more on this in the next chapter). A package that is $199.99 or $195 or $200 imparts a subtle psychological difference even if the offering is exactly the same.

With our broad stroke packages and pricing, let's say both of the Photographers in the examples above specialize primarily in Business Headshots.

Here it is essential and ideally easy to recognize that the Photographer selling a $2,085 Package Two-Headshot Session is targeting a different type of Clientele than the Photographer selling a $525 Package Two-Headshot Session.

However you may feel about either price point, the fact is both can be sold as long as the right demographics are marketed to, an effective sales funnel is in place, and, of course, the product provides value well beyond the amount paid.

So our next step in the process is to fine-tune the products we are offering and then clearly define who would be interested in these products.

It's worthwhile to mention here that you can save yourself a lot of time and heartache by first looking at what products are actually needed rather than creating a product and trying to find your audience afterward.

Like most things in business, there is no shortcut here. If you want to find a product gap, or need, or problem that's currently not being filled in the Photography realm, this means going on social media and reading the threads and identifying people's pain points that are going unanswered.

Then create your product that solves their problem, get it in front of them, and you are off to the races. Of course, this is much easier written than done, and finding out those product gaps will take time.

The other option is you have a product that you alone can create, and you spend your time searching for people who are just as passionate about your product as you are, so passionate that they are willing to spend their time and money to obtain it. This, of course, also happens all the time, though finding the market that loves your product and getting in front of them is what will take time.

This brings us to the quote from entrepreneur Pat Flynn:

The riches are in the niches …[xvii]

This also segues into a great place to mention Entrepreneur.com, one of our most favorite resources. Here you will find a wealth of information and tips on running a business. Part of the creative and fun part of building your business involves learning what other entrepreneurs from different fields have employed effectively and applying those methods to your own company with your own unique spin customized to your own Clientele.

Now back to niches. If you think about it, Specialists are held with a certain regard because they are experts in their particular field, and they are compensated (read: paid) accordingly. A brain surgeon is paid more than a general practitioner. A professor of economics earns more than a high school teacher who teaches a bit of everything. A lawyer specializing in corporate tax law earns more than a solicitor who practices a little bit of everything. The flip side of this is that the demand for Specialists is somewhat less. The Specialist makes up for fewer jobs or Clients by charging more.

As a Photographer, you can offer a wide range of Photography Sessions: corporate headshots, high school portraits, sports photography, weddings, newborns, boudoir, branding, musicians, ... And maybe you can create stunning Images in each and every category.

If you're planning to shoot more and charge less, then you're building what is called a volume business, and most likely you will need to offer a wide range of types of photography.

On the other hand, if you are planning to charge more and shoot less, then you're more likely building what is known as a niche business, think: destination wedding Photographer.

As smartphone cameras continue to improve and the photography industry becomes even more saturated, it might not be overstating it to say that a niche is necessary to build a sustainable business.

Furthermore, with the onset of AI, it is crucially important to create a specialty in an art form that a computer system or robot cannot do.

We believe there still will be a market of folks who appreciate the skills an actual professional Photographer has to offer, and hopefully, we still have some time before people engage AI or robots to photograph their weddings or newborns, though the headshot market is already experiencing the ramifications of this new technology.

So even if you only offer a niche as one particular product stream, it is a good idea to provide some type of photography you specialize in.

There is an incredible variety of niches in photography, limited only to your own creativity.

Sample niches include:

- 360-degree product photos
- Abstract photography that looks like paintings
- Aerial photography
- Alaska imagery
- Americana
- Animals
- Antarctica
- Architectural photography
- Asia-Pacific travel destinations
- Astrophotography
- Automotive photography
- Babies

- Birds
- Birth photography
- Bottle (yes, just bottles, and every kind of bottle)
- Boudoir portraits
- Construction time lapse photography
- Corporate events
- Cultures and environments at risk
- Dating profile photos
- Daytime long exposure photography
- Destination marketing (think Airbnb photos)
- Dogs
- Endurance sports
- Executive jets
- Fashion
- Film photography (i.e., using actual film, not digital)
- Food
- Golf courses
- Google Street View virtual tours
- Haunt industry
- Hawaii volcanoes
- Headshots (for actors and/or executives)
- Horror photography
- Humor
- Hunting, fishing, camping
- Ice hockey
- Imagery for arts organizations
- Industrial photography
- Jewelry
- Kid products and toys
- Landscapes
- LinkedIn profile pictures
- Liquids
- Medical and health care
- Mining
- Personal vacation photographer
- Pet portraiture

- Quinceañera celebrations
- Real Estate Agent portraits
- Rock concerts
- Rodeos
- Senior portrait photography
- Sweet sixteen celebrations
- The nautical world
- Underwater photography
- Wildlife photography
- Yachts

Thank you Flaunt: https://flauntmydesign.com[xviii]

Cross niching and niching down further, you have, for example:

- The Santa Claus Experience by Foster Fine Art Portraits: www.santaclausexperience.com
- Fairytale Portraits by Enchanted Fairies Magical Fine Art Portraiture: https://enchanted-fairies.com/?location=woodland_hills-ca
- Underwater Maternity Portraits by Liz Harlin Photographic: www.lizharlin.com/unique-maternity-photography-underwater-experience-sunshine-coast

The sky's the limit here. Let your imagination run wild and maybe you'll come up with a brand-new niche that's all your own. Just make sure you're passionate about it.

We believe in the quote inspired by the movie *Field of Dreams.*[xix]

Just be prepared to spend a lot of time and energy in building your niche (baseball field), while sacrificing what seems to be a ready-made income generator (corn/Business Portraits), and mixing in sometimes dubious faith and an unrelenting willingness to never give up (just like Kevin Costner's character in the movie).

If you build it, they will come.

Now let's look at finding the "They."

Target Market Personas

So, you've decided to specialize in Aerial Clown Photography set against the backdrop of Mount Rushmore. Excellent choice.

Ideally, you already know people that fit in the specialization of your choice.

If you don't happen to know any daredevil clowns with an affinity for traveling to South Dakota, where do you go about finding them? The same place you would go to find your potential Clients in need of Business Headshots, Branding Photography, or Wedding Photography: the Internet.

Before you begin your exhaustive research, let's create your Target Market Persona aka Target Buyer Persona worksheet. It's probably best and easiest to type this up in a document that you can save and reference and pass on during your exit strategy. There are plenty of templates online that you may download and work from. Or you can create your own.

If you already know people in your Target Market, this process is much easier. If not, get ready to dig in.

The more in-depth you go and the more specific you are, the more you will have to work with when you get to the next stages in building your business; these stages will become much easier, and ultimately, this will increase the chances of your business succeeding.

At the top of the page, give your persona a name.

Let's call our first persona: Daredevil Claude.

Or maybe it's Businessman Brad. Or Jack and Jill Newlyweds.

All kidding aside, try to get as specific as possible. Maybe you name your first persona Juan Garcia because you are targeting Hispanic realtors.

Next, create an avatar for this target market persona. Either create one or if you know someone in your demographic, use their photo (even if you didn't take it). The point here is to really bring into focus the Clients you want to attract.

Now it's time to really get to know them. Do this by answering the following questions in relation to the service you will be offering them. If you don't have an answer for any of them, do your online research. Look at Facebook, Instagram, X, Reddit, Quora, Yelp, anywhere and everywhere you think they might be.

Have fun with this and really put yourself in their shoes. Again, taking the time to do the work here will pay off in dividends later.

Also, while the term "brand" will come up in the following questions, we will be covering the topic of branding in-depth in Chapter 7.

Here we go:

Persona Name: Avatar Photo:

Age:

Occupation:

Income:

Location: where do they live?

Two-word description of this person:

Quote: If you were them, what would your motto be pertaining to the product or service you will offer them? For example, if you plan to specialize in Family Portraits, Molly Mom's quote might be:

Family portraits are the things I would be truly devastated over losing in a fire. They are an extremely important heirloom to me and I plan to have them taken every year to record my family's history. Or something like that.

Motivations:

Goals:

Frustrations/Obstacles:

Personality Traits:

Demeanor:

Brief Biography:

Business/Industry they are in:

What was their Career Path?

What is their family life like?

How proficient are they in using technology?

What brands inspire them? Insert the logos of those brands here

Communication preferences:

How can you access them?

What problem or problems do they face?

What keeps them up at night?

What can you do:

    To help your persona achieve their goals?

    To help your persona overcome their challenges?

What solution can you offer?

    Why would they be coming to your web page?

    What are they expecting from your page?

Common Objections:

    Why wouldn't they buy your product or service?

    What motivates their buying decisions?

Feel free to add more questions, even more specific questions, like what's their astrological sign, their favorite meal, their favorite movie, and so on.

Real-Life Quotes:

Ideally something someone you know actually said about their problem and how your product specifically solves it.

These can become testimonials for you to publish on your marketing materials by asking permission from the person who said it first.

One- to Two-Sentence Brief Description:

Juan Garcia is between the ages of 30 and 40 years. He is a Hispanic realtor serving the Hispanic market of people looking for homes in Pasadena in the $300,000 to $500,000 range. He is married, most likely has children between the ages of <1 year old and 18+. He makes $75,000 on average per year, and he values family. He spends his free time with his wife and kids engaging in fun activities. His favorite brands are Disney and Home Depot.

We wrote the above without any research. Again, use the research you conduct to really get to know this persona. Know them so well that you can begin answering the next question in the language they would actually use.

What is a day in their life like?

Write out a typical day in your persona's life. Write it in the first person as if you are them, and describe their activities and feelings from the moment they wake up to the moment they go to sleep.

Next, it's time to look at your competition. By researching other Photographers in your niche and area, you will uncover valuable info about what to offer in packages, how your pricing compares to their packages, and how they are presenting their packages, pricing, and, ultimately, their business.

This is not an intimation to copy their packages, pricing, and marketing. It is a suggestion to analyze your competition to find out:

What Clients are they targeting?
What problems are they solving?
In what areas are they lacking?

Then brainstorm on how to improve on that. Do not get discouraged or overconfident here. Again, take out the emotion and simply evaluate what's currently available.

Now let's turn our attention to questions about your own business. This is the time to start thinking about your answers, answers that will serve as the basis for your branding and marketing materials.

Marketing Messaging:
How should you describe your solution to your persona?

Elevator Pitch:
An elevator pitch is a brief (think 30 seconds) way of introducing yourself, getting across a key point or two about your business, and making a connection with someone. It's called an elevator pitch because it takes roughly the amount of time you'd spend riding in an elevator with someone.[xx] (Thanks Princeton University!)

Use your elevator pitch to tell your persona about your solution.

Your Unique Selling Proposition (USP):
How are you different from the competition, and why is this relevant to Clients?

What is the specific and unique benefit to choosing you over the competition?

Why do your Clients care about this benefit?

What is the one benefit you offer that your Target Client values above all others?

Now, do this whole process again for **each and every single Client** you plan to serve. If you're also offering business headshots and wedding packages, then do this for Brad Businessman and Jack and Jill Newly-weds, along with every other persona you hope to have as your Client.

(If you would like a copy of our Target Market Persona Question-naire Template in Google Docs or Word format, please e-mail us at: natasha@markmaryanovich.com with the subject line Templates, and we'll be happy to send one along!)

We cannot emphasize enough how much the more detailed work you do here, the more it will pay off later. Going back to the seed analogy, you may feel at this point that this is an exercise in redundant busy work, the point where all you see is just dirt, and sometimes it's manure. Only until much later, a tuft of green appears and it begins to flourish.

Though you can easily count the seeds in an apple, you can't count the apples in a seed.[xxi]

—Unknown

CHAPTER 7

The Client Experience

As we continue to work backward, we're led to the Client Experience. Yes, we haven't tackled marketing yet, or sales, though none of the work you put into those facets will matter if the experience you provide your Client after you've marketed to and sold them is less than amazing.

In today's day and age, with social media and online reviews, and the proliferation of entrepreneurship, it's no longer enough to just "wow" Clients. Ideally you want to provide an experience that "Woah ..."s them. As in "Woah, that was AMAZING!!"[xxii]

Because you've done the hard work of really getting to know and understand your Client, you will be able to craft an experience from start to finish that knocks them off their feet.

Basically it comes down to this:

Treat others the way they want to be treated.[xxiii]

—(The Platinum Rule) popularized
by Dr. Tony Alessandra and Dr. Michael J. O'Connor

If there are some gaps where you may not know exactly what it is that will "Woah" each of your Clients specifically, then two more quotes come to mind:

You know what that means? (Pointing to the Temet Nosce sign.)
It's Latin. It means know thy self.[xxiv]

—Oracle from *The Matrix*

Do to others what you would have them do to you.[xxv]

—(The Golden Rule) Matthew 7:12; Luke 6:31

If ever you're stuck on how to deal with a Client (or anyone for that matter), always ask yourself: how would I want to be treated? What would I want to hear? What would I want to experience?

This brings us to our next recommended reading: *How To Win Friends And Influence People* by Dale Carnegie. This book can and should change your life and how you run your business. Please read and enjoy.

Once you've finished reading *How To Win Friends …* you'll know one of the many truths Dale Carnegie filled this book with. At heart, we're not so different, you and I. Being brought up and living under the exact same circumstances with the exact same experiences, I would be you, and you would be me.

Think about it. If you've been fortunate to have an experience where a business "Woah"s you, you cannot help but share that experience with your friends, family, even mild acquaintances and strangers, if the "Woah" was big enough. And usually, we share these experiences completely un-provoked. Not when asked, or when relevant to the conversation. We just can't help but share what made us go "Woah."

This is the kind of marketing we want. It's free, it's convincing, and it creates repeat Clients and referrals.

So rather than spending time on quirky marketing and publicity stunts or trying to go viral, spend time creating an exceptional "Woah"-based Client experience.

How do you do that? You start by listing out your touchpoints.

Your touchpoints are every and any way Clients "can interact with a business organization, whether person-to-person, through a website, an app or any form of communication. … When (Clients) connect with these touchpoints they can consider their perceptions of the business and form an opinion."[xxvi] (Thanks again Wikipedia!)

For example:

A Client calls or e-mails you or texts you about a potential Photo-shoot. Your response (including length of time before you respond, how you respond, in what method you respond, the info you provide when you respond)—that's a touchpoint.

A Client decides to go ahead and book you. The way this booking is confirmed: sending the contract, the contract itself, your invoicing system, your invoice itself, how you accept payment, what happens after you receive their payment—these are all touchpoints.

The lead-up to their Session Day: do they hear from you beforehand? If so, that's a touchpoint.

The Session Day—that's a touchpoint.

How you request and accept their balance payment and what happens after they send their balance payment—touchpoint, touchpoint, touchpoint.

Delivering their Gallery of Images—you got it, that's a touchpoint.

After their Photoshoot: do they hear from you again? If so, say it with me: that's a touchpoint.

So have some fun, get creative, and list out all the touchpoints you will have with your Client. Again, it's a good idea to work backward from after their shoot day to the stage when they are just inquiring, then, after reading the upcoming section on branding, dream up ways to "Woah" them every step of the way.

Client Onboarding

In creating your list of touchpoints, you'll want to define your Client onboarding experience, that is, how you will explain your processes (e.g., payment terms, Image delivery, and so on) to your new Clients. In short, what they can expect from working with you.

Here you want to set clear expectations so that you can utilize another tenet of business: underpromise and overdeliver. This sets you on your way to "Woah"-ing your Client. What does this mean?

Tell them you'll have their Gallery ready in three days and have it ready in one day (for example). Tell them their package includes 50 Images, and deliver 75. Like that.

This brings us to discounts, refunds, cancellations, and Image delivery. During the process of determining your Client touchpoints, you will want to consider how you will handle these important aspects of your Client experience.

If you so choose to offer discounts and/or accept a Photoshoot at a discounted rate, be sure to go back to your COGS and O&GE and make absolutely sure you are not going out-of-pocket (i.e., losing money) to work with someone before you agree to do the shoot.

Determine the maximum discount you can give, while still at the very least breaking even (if, for example, it affords you the chance to work with a Client you really want to work with). If possible, factor discounts into your pricing at the outset so that when you do offer your discount (perhaps as part of a last resort closing technique, more on this later) this discount will not affect your profit margin.

How you handle refunds and cancellations is up to you, again, based on your COGS and O&GE, and again, on what you yourself would think is noble and fair. Clearly explain your refund and cancellation policies on your website's FAQs page, in your contract, and your invoices, and on any other place in your Client onboarding material. It cannot be overstated: your Client must understand your stance on this at all times.

They must also understand your terms regarding when exactly they will receive their Images. We highly recommend that they receive their Images as soon as their balance has been paid. Not before and not too long after. Trying to collect payment after the customer has already received their goods is not the norm in many, many, many businesses, and it shouldn't be in yours.

There is, however, an exception to every rule, and perhaps one of your Clients consistently hires you throughout the years and pays you above your book rate—then maybe you want to send them their Gallery and collect payment afterward, as part of your process of "Woah"-ing them. This is up to you, and you must be okay with the fact that maybe you won't receive that balance, for whatever reason.

Here it is worthwhile to mention the following touchpoint you should include that doesn't directly relate to your Clients' interaction with your business; it's more about your interaction with your Clients:

Do your research about your Client (their background, family, where they're coming from, and so on). Find out as much as you can without stalking them. Nothing sours a shoot more than asking a question about something you should already know, or saying something that offends them. Do your homework. Know your Clients.

The following story comes from Nikki Nash's *Market Your Genius*.[xxvii] In her brilliant book, she talks about a highly successful barber and businessman. His success stems from getting to know his Clients:

If they love drinking a certain type of soda, he always has it in his shop during their appointments. If they wanted to drink champagne while getting a haircut, he made sure they had champagne. He treated his Clients like kings and queens. Then eventually, they'd ask how they could help him. He would ask them to bring a friend. It's that simple: "I kissed their asses and asked them to bring more asses in the door."

If kissing asses or treating people like royalty isn't your vibe, then you should probably think about spending your time doing something other than running a business.

The fact is your Clients deserve to be treated like kings and queens. They deserve to be treated like gold. Not only are they trusting you with an experience a lot of people compare with going to the dentist—an experience in which they might feel vulnerable, and ultimately forces them to face their self-image, they are trusting you with their hard-earned money.

More than that, they are trusting you with their time.

There's a reason the word "spend" is used with both money and time. Time is unequivocally more valuable than money. We can't make more of it, we actually get less of it.

If you literally count the minutes and hours one has out of an unknown quantity of time, the choice your Clients are making to spend them with you—instead of with their family or friends or on a well-loved hobby, or other new experience—is an honor they're bestowing upon you.

On top of this, they are putting food on your table, valuing your creative work, and allowing you the freedom and great fortune to be able to continue to run your own business and be your own boss, something many people only dream of.

So treat them like royalty and make them go "Woah." They more than deserve it.

This brings us to Branding.

The number of blog posts, books, articles, podcasts, webisodes, and video tutorials on branding seems endless. Feel free to spend days, weeks, or months learning all you can about it. Here, we're going to try and keep things simple.

Sometimes, when we hear people talking about branding, it makes us remember the character Inigo Montoya played by Mandy Patinkin in *The Princess Bride*.

Wallace Shawn plays the Sicilian boss Vizzini, who frequently uses the word "inconceivable" to describe events. Eventually, Montoya says to him, "You keep using that word. I do not think it means what you think it means."[xxviii] This is sometimes how we feel when people use the word "brand" or "branding."

At its most basic level, branding is the perception of your business that exists in people's minds. It's how they feel or think about your company.

Again, bring it back to yourself. What thoughts come to mind when you see the Apple logo? How do you feel when you see the Nike swoosh?

Branding is the process of using your designs (including your logo), mission statement (more on this in Chapter 10), and marketing messages (more on this in Chapter 9) to *influence* how people think and feel about your business.

The colors you select, the words you use, the Images you present all create the perception of your business. After all, these are the only things someone will see when first becoming aware and then getting to know your company. So select them carefully, after you've decided how you want to make people feel.

Go back to your Target Market Personas and use the answers you've come up with as the basis for creating your brand.

You want to choose colors and designs that will appeal to your personas, and you'll also want to use the same words and language that they use in your written content.

To start this process, open up a new document and begin to build your Brand Pyramid[xxix]:

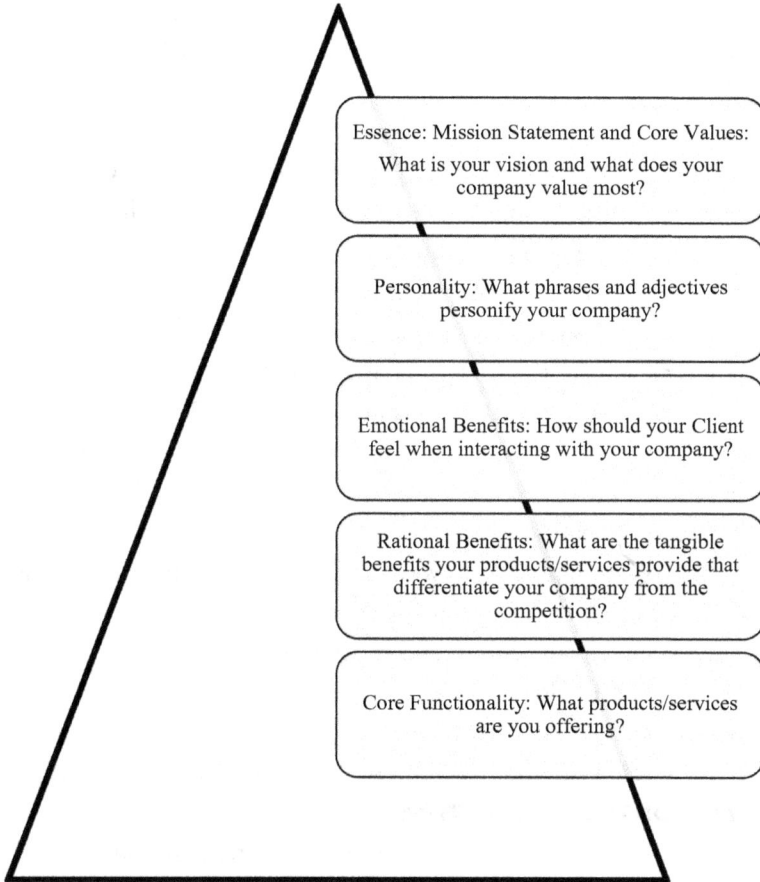

Figure 7.1 Brand Pyramid

Next, work on your brand promise. This is like a pledge: What are you and your company dedicated to providing to your Target Market Persona?

Now you're going to work on your Positioning Statement. Here you'll want to clarify your USP (Unique Selling Proposition): essentially what makes you different from all the other Photographers out there. Why will working with you be different and more preferable to potential Clients?

Side note: This may include applying for awards in hopes of winning, though keep in mind, many contests charge entry fees, and if you plan to include this in your strategy, budget this in your marketing plan (more on this later) and set a cap on how many contests you will enter, and how much you will spend on entry fees.

After you've completed these steps, distill everything you've come up with about what makes you unique in what you do for your Clients into one succinct sentence. This is known as your Tag Line. Ideally it becomes something that makes sense to use in all your social media profile descriptions and prominently on your website, your business card, the bottom of your e-mails, and so on.

This might take time. Days, weeks, months, even years to perfect. Don't let this hold you back from launching though. Business is a process of iteration. You won't know what works until you present it in the real world, and only then can you improve based on the feedback your Clients and potential Clients are giving you.

Once you've done the hard work of figuring out your brand pyramid, promise, USP and initial tag line, you then *get* to move onto the fun stuff: selecting your colors and fonts and creating your logo.

Again, do this with your Target Market Personas top of mind. There are a lot of resources on the web about color psychology and the feelings each color conveys. Also, you're most likely familiar with the fact that *certain* **FONTS** make **you** feel *differently*.

Decide on fonts and colors that exude the feelings you want your potential Clients to experience when learning about your company.

Choose three colors you'll use consistently throughout your website and marketing materials. If three doesn't seem like enough to you, keep in mind, you can use varying shades of each color.

Then pick two fonts that you'll also consistently use throughout your website and marketing materials.

If you believe you can design a professional logo for yourself, then do it. If not, engage a professional designer. If you don't know any professional designers, then search for one on the Internet and look at their work to see if it resonates with what you have in mind.

Either way, create a logo that embodies your company's style, thoughts, and feelings you want to project.

Now let's think about the words you're going to use in your communications with your Clients and potential Clients, the words you're going to use on your website, marketing materials, social media posts, e-mails, and so on.

It's time to determine your Tone.

Again, go back to the information you unearthed while learning about your Target Market Personas. Will your Personas resonate with humor (always risky as what's funny to one person may be offensive to another), casualness, strict professionalism, or something in-between? Whatever tone you decide to adopt, use it consistently throughout every single sentence you write.

This brings up a long-held truism in business. People do business with people they know, like, and trust. Again, bring it back to you:

- Would you hire (read: give money) to a complete stranger vs. someone you've heard great things about?
- Would you hire (read: give money) to someone you dislike vs. someone you think the world of?
- Would you hire (read: give money) to someone you don't trust?

This is where consistency comes in. Today, a lot of relationships begin and are built up based on words alone: e-mails, text messages, social media posts, blogs, and websites.

You need to use your words to get people to know you, then like you, then trust you. Any inconsistency in language and tone will breed a certain level of distrust.

So pick a tone and stick with it.

Finally, in this introduction to branding, the last element we'll look at is your Brand Image. This is the photo you'll be using for all of your social media profile pictures and on your website, maybe even at the bottom of your e-mails and on your business card.

As a Photographer, this Image of course needs to be top-notch, and it also needs to portray the feelings you want people to have when they consider your company. As the face of your business, this photo will most likely be of you. Though again, keep branding in mind. Maybe a photo of your dog who looks like you wearing sunglasses embodies the exact message you want to broadcast if you are a pet portrait Photographer. Or maybe your baby picture is what you want to present if you're a newborn Photographer. The point here is to get creative and have fun in creating ways that your brand will broadcast all the amazing ways that you stand out in the field of Photography.

With a grasp on your brand, it's now time to go back to your touch-points and craft all the ways you will "Woah" your Clients, ways that stem from and exude the thoughts and feelings you want your Clients to have throughout the entire process of working with you and your business.

It is also helpful to now create templates for all the ways you plan to "Woah" your Clients (e.g., templates for your e-mails, phone scripts, text messages, and so on) so you can ensure each and every one of them receives the same amazing experience each and every time, each and every step of the way.

CHAPTER 8

Sales

Continuing along our work backward plan, we're now going to look at sales. Yes, sales before marketing, and yes, sales is a completely different entity from marketing.

Marketing is the various activities you will do to make people aware of your business, that is, generate leads.

A lead, according to Investopedia, is a person who may eventually become a Client.[xxx]

business.adobe.com identifies a lead as someone who has simply identified themselves as someone who wants more information.[xxxi]

Either way, your goal is to turn leads into paying Clients once they become aware. The process of turning leads into Clients—people that book and pay you—is sales.

Every person that becomes aware or inquires about your business won't necessarily hire you, not immediately anyways. So the challenge here is to come up with a sales process that will increase the amount of leads that will book you.

We're starting with sales because no matter how many people you make aware of your business (e.g., bring to your website or get to call you/contact you to inquire about your services)—all of these leads, time, energy, and money (if you've paid for a marketing tactic) will be wasted if you do not have an effective sales process in place.

This is often referred to as your Sales Funnel or Sales Pipeline. Figure this out first before spending countless hours and dollars on blog posts, e-mail marketing, or paying for ads both online and off.

While we mentioned at the start of this book that the fundamentals of business rarely change dramatically, what does change extremely rapidly is what techniques will work in getting people to respond and buy your products or services.

A few short years ago everyone wanted content, content, content. Lists and how-tos and guides on everything and anything related to your product or service or industry or problem you solve. Now, everyone is on information overload, and the last thing people want is another whitepaper.

Whitepaper: an informational document that gives an in-depth analysis of a subject while highlighting a business's products or services and encouraging people to use them.[xxxii] (Thanks Mailchimp!)

So creativity comes into play here too. You'll need to come up with strategies that get people to click Book Now/Pay Now (not Contact Now, that's marketing) at each stage of your funnel[xxxiii]:

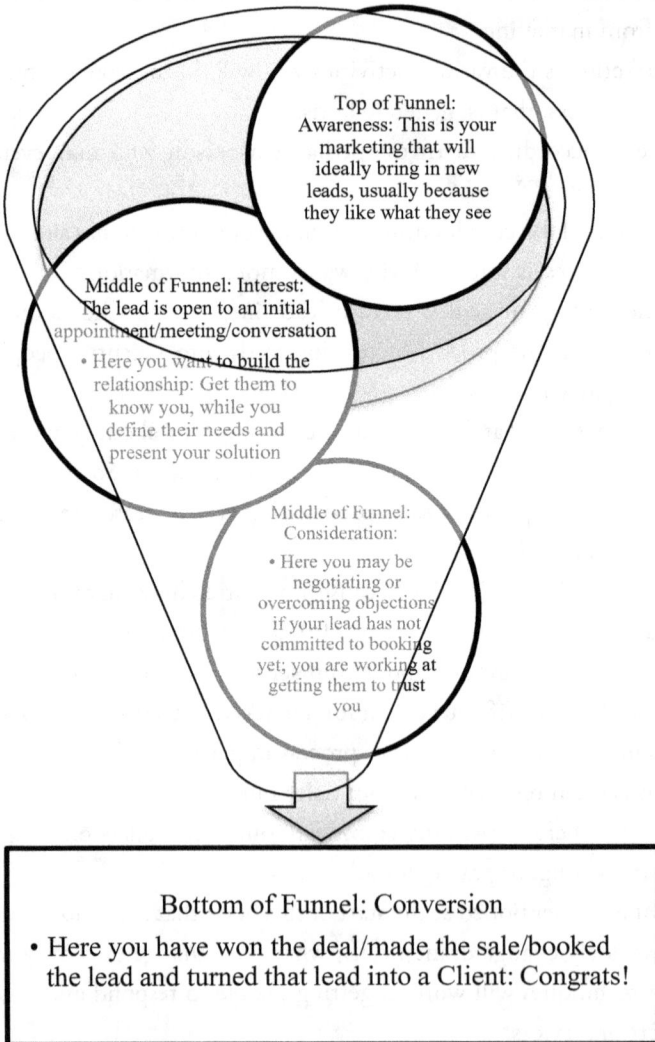

Top of Funnel:
Awareness: This is your marketing that will ideally bring in new leads, usually because they like what they see

Middle of Funnel: Interest: The lead is open to an initial appointment/meeting/conversation

• Here you want to build the relationship: Get them to know you, while you define their needs and present your solution

Middle of Funnel: Consideration:

• Here you may be negotiating or overcoming objections if your lead has not committed to booking yet; you are working at getting them to trust you

Bottom of Funnel: Conversion

• Here you have won the deal/made the sale/booked the lead and turned that lead into a Client: Congrats!

Figure 8.1 Sales Funnel

Since we've reached the bottom of the funnel, now is a good time to discuss Conversions. While what will work to get people to buy often changes drastically on almost a weekly basis, age-old "closing techniques" (i.e., closing the deal) that have worked for decades are helpful to look at. Here's a list provided by ChangingMinds.org.[xxxiv] See if you can recognize which ones have worked on you any time you've bought something:

1-2-3 Close—close with the principle of three

Adjournment Close—give them time to think

Affordable Close—ensure people can afford what you are selling

Alternative Close—offer a limited set of choices

Artisan Close—show the skill of the designer

Ask-the-Manager Close—use manager as authority

Assumptive Close—act as if they are ready to decide

Balance Sheet Close—add up the pros and the cons

Best Time Close—emphasize how now is the best time to buy

Bonus Close—offer delighter to clinch the deal

Bracket Close—make three offers—with the target in the middle

Calculator Close—use calculator to do discount

Calendar Close—put it in the diary

Companion Close—sell to the person with them

Compliment Close—flatter them into submission

Concession Close—give them a concession in exchange for the close

Conditional Close—link closure to resolving objections

Cost of Ownership Close—compare cost over time with competitors

Courtship Close—woo them to the close

Customer Care Close—the Customer Care Manager calls later and reopens the conversation

Daily Cost Close—reduce cost to daily amount

Demonstration Close—show them the goods

Diagram Close—draw a picture that draws them in

Distraction Close—catch them in a weak moment

Doubt Close—show you doubt the product and let them disagree

Economic Close—help them pay less for what they get

Embarrassment Close—make not buying embarrassing

Emotion Close—trigger identified emotions

Empathy Close—empathize with them, then sell to your new friend

Empty Offer Close—make them an empty offer that the sale fills

Exclusivity Close—not everyone can buy this

Extra Information Close—give them more info to tip them into closure

Fire Sale Close—focus on soiled goods, going cheap

Future Close—close on a future date

Give-Take Close—give something, then take it away

Golden Bridge Close—make the only option attractive

Goldilocks Close—give three options, with the middle option being best

Handover Close—someone else does the final close

Handshake Close—offer handshake to trigger automatic reciprocation

Humor Close—relax them with humor

Hurry Close—go fast to stop them thinking too much

IQ Close—say how this is for intelligent people

Minor Points Close—close first on the small things

Never-the-best-time Close—focus on no time is best for customers who are delaying

No-hassle Close—make it as easy as possible

Now-or-never Close—focus on time running out to hurry things up

Opportunity Cost Close—show the cost of not buying

Ownership Close—act as if they own what you are selling

Price Promise Close—promise to meet any other price

Puppy Close—acting cute to invoke sympathy and a nurturing response

Quality Close—sell on quality, not on price

Rational Close—use logic and reason

Repetition Close—repeat a closing action several times

Requirements Close—write down what they want as a formal requirement

Retrial Close—go back to square one

Reversal Close—act as if you do not want them to buy the product

Save-the-world Close—buy now and help save the world

Selective-deafness Close—respond only to what you want to hear

Shame Close—make not buying shameful

Shopping List Close—tick off list of their needs

Similarity Close—bond them to a person in a story

Standing-room-only Close—show how others are lined up to buy

Summary Close—tell them all the things they are going to receive

Testimonial Close—use a happy customer to convince the new customer

Thermometer Close—ask on a scale of 1 to 10 how likely they are to buy, then based on their number and reason for that number, you close the gap

Think About It Close—give them time to think about it

Treat Close—persuade them to "give themselves a treat"

Trial Close—see if they are ready for a close

Valuable Customer Close—offer them a special "VIP" deal

Ultimatum Close—show negative consequences of not buying

Yes-Set Close—get them saying "yes" and they'll keep saying "yes"

More information about each technique can be found at: https://changingminds.org/disciplines/sales/closing/closing_techniques.htm (Thanks ChangingMinds.org!)

Now that you've seen the funnel from top to bottom, here's an example sales funnel you're most likely familiar with:

- You see an ad online out of the corner of your eye: Awareness.
- You click on it, and it leads you to a company's website where a pop-up window comes up asking for your e-mail address in exchange for something this website will give you: 10 percent off your next purchase, a free sales funnel template download, and so on. You get sucked in, you enter your e-mail address: Interest.
- You receive your 10 percent discount code/coupon or template along with an invite to schedule a free consultation on how this website's product can solve your problem; you accept the invitation: Consideration.
- Suddenly, you're on a Zoom call with one of the company's sales reps listening to all the positive benefits their product

will bring to your life. Any time you hesitate, the salesperson has a quick response: Negotiating and Overcoming Objections.

- You continue to resist, so the salesperson goes into action employing one of the closing techniques listed earlier. You're so convinced you decide to buy and give the company your credit card info: Conversion.

Now it's time to create your own funnel. At each stage along this funnel, you *get* to craft strategies that will encourage the lead to take the next step, then the next step, then the next step until they are booked.

Each strategy and each step needs to embody your brand's promise, positioning, tone, and style. A 10 percent discount coupon might not necessarily jive if you're a luxury brand trying to appeal to elegant Clients. Not all Target Personas will want a free consultation, especially via Zoom.

Here again, the information you uncovered during your Target Market Persona research should guide you.

Going back to Pat Flynn's citation on riches and niches, the second part of his quote is:

… the fortune is in the follow-up.[xxxv]

Sales follow-ups are an art in and of themselves, and a large part of what changes drastically in terms of what motivates people to buy is their receptivity to subsequent selling interactions.

At one point, the rule of thumb was to follow-up no sooner than 5 business days from the initial outreach. In our current world, a lot can happen in 5 days, and people often need a reminder much sooner than that. However, follow-up too soon and you risk irritating your potential Client. Follow-up too late and they may have moved on to someone else.

It's a fine balance to determine when and how you should follow up, and while some modern research suggests that an average consumer needs to hear about or from a business seven to eight times before actually purchasing,[xxxvi] other research contends that repetition of the same message could have a negative impact instead of a positive one.[xxxvii]

The takeaway from the statement above is "the same message." Make sure that if you do decide to follow up, whether it be three or eight times or any number in between, you are providing new and valuable information that is useful to your potential Client each and every single time.

Sales is certainly a specialty and that's why the top "closers" in any industry earn more than $100,000 per year. If you do decide to hire a closer, make sure they are clear on your brand values, tone, and style.

If you're planning on tackling sales yourself, mindset is crucially important here.

A Man Without a Smiling Face Must Not Open a Shop!
—Chinese proverb

Nikki Nash from *Market Your Genius* goes so far as to suggest creating a playlist of songs that empower and inspire you and to play this list before engaging in the process of converting a lead to a Client, be it by phone, e-mail, Zoom, or face-to-face meeting.[xxxviii]

If the whole idea of sales makes your skin crawl, then you'll need to take a good look at why you're doing this whole business building thing in the first place, and then reframe your perspective.

If you've made it this far and still want to continue to be a professional Photographer, it's most likely because you believe your photos are worth being paid for, that is, worth being bought and sold.

If you don't believe in your product, then you really need to think about why you want to build a business.

Ideally, you believe your photos are worth being paid for because they bring value to the life of the person who pays for them.

If, after figuring out your USP and positioning, you still don't know the value you provide, know this:

You will only begin to make money, sustainable business money, once you offer something of value: a valuable experience, service, or product.

So go back, figure this out, and once you know it, focus on this, as a salesperson is absolutely more successful when they believe in their product and understand and can clearly communicate the value it will bring to someone's life.

In terms of reframing your perspective, if you approach your sales process as service, and truly serving your Client, then you will have much more success. No under-handed or strong-armed tactics here. Today's consumer knows when they're being worked, hustled, and sold. And they do not like it. (Do you?) Utilizing any strategy that is less than honorable will not work, especially in the long run, full stop.

When a person is effective at sales, it's a win-win for everyone involved. You're never trying to pull one over a Client, or give them the short end of the stick. Running your business in this way will run it straight into the ground.

Also, never go for the short money. In other words, don't make a money grab in your first interaction with a Client, or any interaction for that matter. You want to build a relationship with your Clients so that you have the fortunate blessing of working with them many times throughout your career. You want to "Woah" them every step of the way and continually "Woah" them so they will keep coming back and tell their friends.

What you want ultimately is a business based on repeat Clients and referrals. It's a well-known maxim in business that it costs less to keep a Client than to find a new one. It's a maxim because it's true. You'll need to spend time and money on continually marketing and finding new leads, courting them to become Clients and then educating them about the process of working with you if each Client you have chooses never to work with you again. And if your Clients are choosing to never work with you again, then this is a giant red flag that needs attention.

If your business is based on serving the same Clients each year or so, the process will be much more enjoyable for both you and your Clients.

So make yourself available to genuinely and authentically serve your Client in every and any aspect you can identify to keep them coming back.

Do they need help with their wardrobe? Then you provide that service. Do they need help choosing a frame? Then you are more than happy to make suggestions and guide them. Do they need help hanging their wall art you created for them? Then you will provide that service or arrange for a professional to do so. Serve, serve, serve.

A friend of ours recently got into an altercation as she made her way home from her mother's 80th birthday celebration. Our friend has been taking photography lessons online and captured the entire party. While she was waiting for the train, someone approached her and tried to grab her luggage. In that moment, as her bags were almost being snatched away, the only thing that concerned her—not the potential threat of bodily harm or to her life, or losing her wallet, credit cards, passport, ID—was that she did not want to lose her camera and the Images still on the card within it.

This is the importance of Photography and the value people place upon it.

CHAPTER 9

Marketing

Alright, we've made it through to marketing. This is where the job gets fun.

A quick and vital pit stop here: Marketing Math.[xxxix]

Now that you ideally have a solid sales funnel in place to book the number of Photoshoots you want to each year, it's time to fill in the following equation with the numbers that make sense to you.

These numbers will come from:

a. Looking at your existing data that you will have hopefully recorded somewhere

b. Going back and figuring out this data by looking at the dates the Client initially contacted you (ideally you recorded it in your calendar system) or finding a text message or e-mail living in your phone or computer

c. Estimating a plausible number if you have no data to base this on

Example 1:

- Your business plans to sell one Photoshoot per week
  = Four Photoshoots per month
- On average it takes 4 months from first contact to closing a lead
  (4 months is completely arbitrary here, your amount of months could be much more or less, depending on how effective your sales funnel is, the type of photography you provide, and the products you offer)
- One out of four leads eventually becomes a Client, meaning you have a close ratio of 25 percent (exceptional*)
  Therefore, the math is this:

- 4 Photoshoots × 4 months/25 percent close ratio = 64 leads
  In this example, you need 64 active leads at all times to increase your chances of closing four Clients per month.

Example 2:

- Your business plans to sell four Photoshoots per week
  = 16 Photoshoots per month
- On average it takes 4 months from first contact to closing a lead
- One out of four leads still eventually becomes a Client, meaning you have a close ratio of 25 percent (still exceptional*) Therefore, the math is this:
- 16 Photoshoots × 4 months/25 percent close ratio =
  256 leads
  In this example, you need 256 active leads at all times to increase your chances of closing 16 Clients per month.

With this math, you can now set quantifiable goals for your marketing. Thanks BDC!

*According to Dooly.ai[xl] "High-performing sales organizations are said to close 30% of their sales qualified leads (SQLs), while average companies only close 20%." In reality, while 30 percent may be possible, without engaging an experienced sales professional expect your closing rate to be more like 2 percent to 6 percent, and this is if your sales funnel is strong.

The numbers in the examples above were chosen for simplicity's sake, and also to not discourage you. In today's online world, it is possible for your marketing strategies to generate thousands of leads, and it is possible for you to hit the 30 percent close rate if you are an expert at sales.

Now it's time to start attracting those leads.

Back to marketing. Again, there is a seemingly endless stream of books, blog posts, websites, videos, podcasts, and companies that specialize in this, and there are a ton of tools you can incorporate into your marketing kit. Here, we're covering the basics.

Basic marketing tools include:

- Business cards
- Flyers
- Mailers (physical items you send through the actual mail)
- E-mail marketing
- Blogs
- Vlogs
- Social media posts
- Online ads
- Website

Beyond these, there are things like marketing activities, advertising, publicity, and public relations. Marketing activities are activities you perform solely to generate attention for your business. Think contests, raffles, giveaways, hosting an all-you-can-eat spaghetti ice cream party, like that.

Advertising can include renting billboards, bus benches, and in the olden days paying for magazine and newspaper ads or commercials on the local television network or PBS.

Marketing publicity refers to gaining public visibility or awareness for a product, service, or your company via the media and other communication channels.

Unlike advertising, which is paid, publicity is usually earned and comes about because something about your business is deemed newsworthy.[xli] (Thanks ActiveCampaign!).

Some savvy business owners use their launch as a strategy, sending press releases to the local news outlets to ideally generate interest in having some media outlet cover it (i.e., write about it).

According to Wikipedia (thanks again!), public relations and publicity differ in that "PR is controlled internally, whereas publicity is not controlled and contributed by external parties."[xlii]

The Public Relations Society of America defines PR as "a strategic communication process that builds mutually beneficial relationships between organizations and their publics."[xliii]

Whatever strategies and tactics you so choose to employ, keep in mind that each and every one should bring value to your potential Client and Client's lives.

If you choose to use e-mail marketing, please know that everyone is tired of the newsletter that asks the recipient to "check this out" or "visit my store" or "watch this video." No one has the time or patience today.

If you are sending out content that you hope will help your readers, consider this: Which would you prefer reading?

"The Complete How-To Guide To Styling Your Hair For A Photoshoot" (10-minute read)

Or

"The Magic Wand That Will Style Your Hair Photoshoot Ready In Minutes" (2-minute read)

Most likely, you would prefer option two. If so, then it's probably safe to say a good number of your readers would prefer option two too. So write and send option two and be sure you deliver the magic wand.

A few words on e-mail marketing while we're here. A few very wise business gurus stress the importance of building, maintaining, segmenting, and growing your e-mail list. This is sage advice. A well-kept e-mail subscriber list is gold. These are people who opted in to hearing from you, that is, they want to know more about you and see you in their inbox.

Social media fans and followers are great, until your account gets hacked or that platform disappears.

As important as the e-mail list itself is the proper organization and management of that e-mail list. It is crucial to figure out what system (often referred to as CRM: Customer Relationship Management software) you will use to store your e-mail contacts. Google Contacts can work just fine until you're ready for an all-in-one CRM software like Nutshell, and the monthly fee those services come with.

Decide exactly how you are going to store your contacts from moment one, and moreover, decide how you will segment them.

For instance:

- It's a good idea to segment your leads from your Clients with labels.

- All of your wedding Clients you might want to apply with the label "Wedding Clients."
- All of your Business Headshot Clients you might want to label with "Business Men," "Business Women," "Business They/Them."

Not to touch too much on the gender hot button, the point of segmenting your e-mail list is so that you send the person content that is personalized and specifically useful to them. That is the best way to ensure that they do not hit Unsubscribe.

If you find yourself with 200+ labels and maybe only one to three contacts within each label, this is not OCD in action, it's thorough segmenting. Or so we like to think ☺

Back to marketing.

The bottom line is this: Nobody knows anything and this is especially true when it comes to marketing. No one can predict what's going to go viral or become immensely successful ("Barbenheimer" anyone?), so the real art of marketing is a relentless commitment to trial and error. It's also creating a system to record what does work and what doesn't, and doubling down on what works. Another true maxim of business is what you measure, you can manage.

So come up with a marketing idea, try it, keep track of if it works, that is, how many leads it brought in (how many leads you *booked* is sales), and if it does work, improve what you can and try it again.

Again, marketing is where you get to exercise your creative muscles. The sky is the limit in terms of the techniques you apply and the content you provide. Make it interesting, make it engaging, make it entertaining, and make it valuable, and ideally, make it all of the above and it just might go viral. Another maxim that holds true: good content will always get shared.

Whatever strategies you choose to employ, list them in a spreadsheet, do the research to estimate how much each will cost in terms of time and money, and also list the ROI (Return on Investment) you hope to achieve (i.e., 100 new leads signed up for your e-mail newsletter by the end of the second quarter). Stick to your budget, track the results, and pivot as necessary.

Here, we're going to stick with the basics and the most basic marketing tool you're most likely going to start out with is your website.

You have several options here, in terms of website building and hosting companies. What is important to you as a Photographer is the other features the website building and hosting company provides.

As a Photographer, at minimum, you are going to need:

- A website
- A way to deliver your Images to your Clients, most likely initially as a digital online Gallery from which they can select their favorites and purchase prints if you plan to sell tangible products
- A way for people to book you (i.e., an online scheduling system)
- A way to collect payment

As mentioned in the previous chapter, these are all touchpoints and ideally the programs and processes you use to fulfill the abovementioned needs will "Woah" your Clients.

In terms of collecting payment, it's usually good form to offer your Clients a variety of ways to pay you. Make it easy for them. Again, bring it back to you. Would you rather be able to choose your preferred method of payment, or be told that you can only send payment in the form of coin of the realm via carrier pigeon? Extreme, we know, though hopefully you understand the point.

Photographers are extremely fortunate these days, as there are several companies that offer all-in-one software that handles the facets we need.

For example, Pixieset (https://pixieset.com/pricing) offers not only a customizable website, they also offer a gorgeous online Gallery delivery system, an online shop for print sales, an online booking capability, and the ability to invoice and send digitally signable contracts to your Clients. All in all, an amazing studio management software company, super user-friendly. (We use them, and we love them.) They exist solely for Photographers.

Many of these software companies even provide templates for contracts, releases, and questionnaires with the disclaimer that they are starting points only. Always have a qualified lawyer look over the contracts and releases you will ask your Clients to sign. Contracts and releases are another touchpoint, and while they should include terms pertaining to your payment policies, refunds, rescheduling policies, delivery times, copyright, Image usage, and so on, it's wise to make them as easy to understand as possible for your Clients, and mutually beneficial.

Back to websites and software.

We would be remiss not to mention a couple other amazing studio management software companies currently available:

ShootProof (www.shootproof.com/plans)
Zenfolio (https://zenfolio.com/plans-pricing)

Pixieset's features and design aesthetic fit perfectly with our brand, and in looking at the different options available, you might find that you like the design aesthetics and features of the templates offered by one company and the studio management features offered by another. It happens. Just keep in mind, the fewer platforms you have to learn, then manage, and the fewer monthly or annual bills you have to pay is, of course, preferable.

When you begin the fun journey of building your customizable website, there are two things to understand:

First: construct a site that allows for future growth. Maybe in your 10-year plan, you've envisioned starting a blog, selling wall art, hosting online courses, or providing anything you're presently not offering. If so, leave room to incorporate these elements in a seamless fashion with your current design. It's both time-consuming and deflating when you have to redesign your website from the ground-up in 1 to 2 to 5 years' time when you realize your existing design doesn't fit the direction you would like to go.

Second: your website is not about you. It's about your potential Clients.

Before you start dragging and dropping your Images into a website template builder and filling a text field with info about you, take a look at https://tonicsiteshop.com

Tonic creates customizable templates for Showit, a fully customizable website design software. (We use Showit, we love Showit: https://showit.com) Things to keep in mind with Showit are:

- It's great for SEO (more on this next).
- Fully customizable is a double-edged sword. Just like offering your Clients too many product and service options, having the ability to create almost literally anything you can dream of can cause a lot of confusion and become overwhelming.

This is where Tonic comes in. With the templates they provide, you can simply drag and drop your Images and paste your text into their gorgeous, sales-focused sites, while still utilizing the SEO capabilities Showit offers.

If you can afford the hefty price tags that come with Tonic templates, by all means do it. Their testimonials attest that their websites enable a phenomenal conversion rate and do most of the "closing" for you. If you cannot at this time afford a Tonic site, please sign up for their #longand-weird newsletter from Jen, as not only is it entertaining and funny, it also offers great business advice.

After looking at the Tonic sites, you should realize that your website needs to be a sales tool, as well as a marketing tool. This means you need to have several CTAs (Calls To Action), buttons that leads can click if they want to book you as well as find out more information.

It needs to be more than just a slideshow of your portfolio Images. In fact, your website should contain more words than Images.

What words, you might ask? The words your Target Market Personas use and search for, which brings us to SEO.

Before you embark on the time-intensive task of optimizing your content and site for SEO, we feel obliged to mention that SEO is a long-term strategy; it may be months for the work you implement to take effect and for your site to rank higher on Google, ChatGPT, and/or the current Search Engine dominating the Internet.

What's more, the frequent changes Google makes to its own algorithm, the onset of voice search, and proliferation of AI chat/search-bots all affect SEO, so this work may seem like a complete waste of time.

We believe it's a good idea to learn the basic fundamentals and implement them for two reasons:

1. So that you can benefit from proper SEO and rank higher in the near future (again, it takes time) rather than never, and
2. So that you're not left too far behind the curve as the landscape continually shifts.

Ready to dig in? If so, here we go…

SEO

SEO or Search Engine Optimization at first glance might seem dry and complicated, and it is. The good news is, you only ~~have~~ get to learn the elements once.

SEO "is the art and science of getting web pages to rank higher in search engines such as Google. … Because search is one of the main ways people discover content online, ranking higher in search engines can lead to an increase in traffic to a website."[xliv] (Thanks Optimizely!)

Again, there are seemingly endless blog posts, web pages, podcasts, videos, books, and companies that cover this topic. Here we're going to establish the basics.

Basically, Google and the other search engines use what are often referred to as "spiders" to crawl the Internet day and night 24/7.

According to Google,[xlv] there are two facets to how it (and most likely any search engine) works:

1. Crawling: Google downloads text, images, and videos from pages it finds on the Internet with automated programs called crawlers.
2. Indexing: Google analyzes the text, images, and video files on the page and stores the info in the Google index, which is a (very) large database.

Essentially, Google catalogs and stores info on the web, so it can serve it up in fractions of a second whenever anyone types in or voices what they are looking for (their query).

Being able to show the exact answer to what you're looking for at the top of the Search Engine Results Page (SERP) is what has catapulted Google to its astronomical success and position for world domination.

So SEO has to do with ensuring that your website and all of the content you post on the web (Google takes social media posts, comments, and reactions very seriously) is formatted in a way that the Google bots can understand and categorize correctly.

A quote from Michelle Bali during a Shopify tutorial[xlvi] says it all:

If you want to bury a dead body where no one will find it, put it on the 2nd page of Google.

Again, bring it back to yourself. When searching for something online, do you go through the 2nd and 3rd and 4th … 100th page listings? If you do, you are the exception, not the norm.

Presuming that you are part of the 99 percent of searchers who only look at the first page of Google results,[xlvii] how far do you scroll down the SERP before it overwhelms you and you quickly scroll back to the top to focus on the top three to five listings?

Now, how do you show up in the top three to five listings?

You make sure that when creating your website (and all online content) you are using keywords and keyword phrases.

What are keywords and keyword phrases? This is where your Target Market Persona research comes in.

Keywords and keyword phrases are the words and phrases your Target Market types into the Google search bar, or YouTube search bar, or Instagram search bar, or speaks into their device when looking for the products and services you have to offer.

For example, your Target Market Daredevil Claude might say/type in "photographers specializing in aerial clown photography set against the backdrop of Mount Rushmore" when looking for someone who provides these services.

Ideally, these words and this exact phrase is somewhere on your website so that your link comes up in the search engine results at the top of the page. If there happens to be a lot of other Photographers who specialize in this sort of thing, then the content on your website and other online posts needs to contain words and Images that tell the Google bots exactly why you should be listed above all others.

This is where content like testimonials, reviews, and articles you write and post on how your service is superlative (be it by providing additional resources like the best parachutes to pack, the most aerodynamic costumes to wear, the best midair poses, and so on, or your list of FAQs that clearly explains what the process will be like to work with you) comes into play.

More likely, your Target Market personas will be searching for (your city) Business Headshot photographer, Branding photographer (in your city), Actor Headshots (your city), Wedding photographers who specialize in tattooed brides (in your city). Use these words on your website.

There are many, many tools on the Internet such as Google Ads Keyword Planner that will help you find related keywords and keyword phrases.

Before you begin your related keywords and phrases research, the important part is that you hone in and get really specific on your seed keywords as determined by your Target Market Personas.

For example, there is a vast difference between the type of person searching for:

cheap headshots near me

or

affordable headshots (your city)

and

High End headshots (your city)

Which type of person is your Target Market Persona? Once you're clear on this, then use that exact keyword and keyword phrase to find more related keywords and keyword phrases.

Once you have your list of terms you'd like to rank for, it's time to start peppering them into all of your content.

Now, it is crucial to bring up keyword stuffing, and why you want to avoid it. The Google bots are smart, very smart, and growing smarter with

AI. Google's main concern (brand promise) is to provide an excellent user experience. They are wise to sites that use the phrase "greatest Photographer in the world" in every place it can live on a website, without any actual proof (i.e., testimonials, reviews, accolades) to back it up. Google would quickly be forgotten if it simply sent a searcher to a site loaded with this phrase only for the user to discover that the Photographer is far from the greatest.

The key to writing with keywords is to use language your intended Target Market Persona knows and uses themselves and to write in a way that will appeal to them (tone). Write for them, don't write for spiders.

So, where does this language go? Here is a list of all the elements that relate to SEO on a typical web page:

The Page Slug:
These are the words that identify your page and come after the .com. For example:

www.yourdomain.com/about-me

About me is the Page Slug. Some people use the slug to include keywords. Do this only if it seems natural and makes sense. For example:

www.yourdomain.com/about-your-city-landscape-photographer-your-name

The example above is probably too long though, try to keep it short and sweet.

The Page Name:
This is the name you give your page when you list it on your website in the menu bar and/or in the footer—wherever you place the clickable link to access it.

Example Page Names Include:

About Me
Portfolios
Pricing
Contact

Yes, the Page Name often becomes the page slug, in lowercase with dashes in between, though some website template builders allow you to change the title or the slug even though they refer to the same page. The choice here is up to you. Why would you want them to be different? To include more keywords, without stuffing.

Now let's look at Page Names using keyword examples:

About Your City Landscape Photographer Your Name
Contact Landscape Photographer Your Name
Landscape Photography Portfolios
Landscape Photography Pricing

So here, you see the danger of keyword stuffing. It's unimaginative and tiring for a user to see the words Landscape Photography/Photographer four times in a menu. This is where your related keyword terms come in, and this is where you need to exercise restraint and common sense. What would annoy you as a visitor to a website like yours? What would you find helpful?

The Page Title:
According to Moz.com, a company that builds SEO tools, a title tag

is an HTML element that specifies the title of a web page. A page's title tag can be displayed as part of the search snippet in a search engine results page (SERP). This element forms the clickable headline for the search result and is important for user experience, SEO, and social sharing. ... A well-crafted page title is crucial for user navigation and SEO, as it accurately represents the content and avoids generic titles that could confuse users.[xlviii] (Thanks Moz!)

Page Titles are also known as "meta titles" or "meta title tags."

Whichever term you use, do not confuse it with the headline you write as text on the page itself. This is known as the H1 (more on this soon), and this may look like a Page Title in non-SEO terms and may not be different from the actual SEO Title, though it is different and can be used to provide even more and additional info to the web crawlers.

If you think SEO is confusing at first, it is. Hang in there.

An example Page Title is this:

<u>Moz - SEO Software for Smarter Marketing</u>

When you click on the Page Title above in the SERP, it leads you to https://moz.com.

If using keywords in your Page Title, or in any of your SEO content, placing keywords at the start of the title tag makes them more effective, both for the bots and for the people searching as people tend to read the first few words first before deciding to read more or scroll down.

Your branding text (i.e., business name) most likely goes last unless you have a well-known brand that people are searching for (think: Nike shoes or Apple laptop).

When we just typed Nike shoes into the Google search bar, this is what came up:

<u>Nike® Official Site - Shop Nike® Shoes</u>

As you can see, the savvy marketer will include a call to action right in the Page Title.

Currently, the limit Google has set is 70 characters (including spaces) for Page Titles. (Yes, even character limits change over the course of time.) Right now, anything beyond 70 characters will get cut off. So stay below 70 characters.

For your enjoyment, this awesome sentence is 64 characters long!

The Meta Description:
This is the short paragraph you see under the Page Title in the Search listings that describes the page content.

Going back to the Moz example, this is what you'll find in the SERP:

<u>Moz - SEO Software for Smarter Marketing</u>
Backed by the largest community of SEOs on the planet, Moz builds tools that make SEO, inbound marketing, link building, and content marketing easy.

What you want to do here is write a Meta Description that is conversational (keeping in mind your brand's Target Market tone). Use keywords sparingly and if they make sense. And if you do use keywords, place them at the start of the description.

The main goal to keep in mind when writing these Meta Descriptions is to craft a paragraph that compels people to click on the link to actually visit the page.

The Google limit for Meta Descriptions is currently 300 to 320 characters including spaces. Again, if your paragraph is over 300 to 320 characters, your description will be cut off.

This paragraph is 334 characters long and will get cut off:

All SEO work and no play makes Jack a dull boy. All SEO work and no play makes Jack a dull boy. All SEO work and no play makes Jack a dull boy. All SEO work and no play makes Jack a dull boy. All SEO work and no play makes Jack a dull boy. All SEO work and no play makes Jack a dull boy. All SEO work and no play makes Jack a dull boy …

A few other things to keep in mind:

You'll want to squeeze every ounce of SEO juice out of your content, so try not to repeat yourself. That is, don't use the exact same words and phrases that are already in your Page Title. There's no need to include your Company Name again in the Meta Description if it's already in the Page Title.

If you were unable to cleverly insert a call to action in your Page Title, make sure you include one in your Meta Description. Again, you're enticing people to click on your link and visit your site.

Furthermore, you're going to ~~have to~~ get to write completely unique and different Page Titles and Meta Description for every single page of your website. Google scorns duplicate content and will actually penalize (read: not list) your website if the crawlers find it on your web pages.

Also, the bots aren't loving non-alphanumeric characters, specifically double quotation marks ("). Single quotation marks (') are fine, and don't cause the bots to stop crawling your content.

In addition, words like "and" "the" "a" "an" "it" "for" "or" "but" "in" "my" "your" "our" and "their" (aka stop words) are skipped over by Google as they are usually not the most important part of what the searcher is searching for.

These words are, however, important for a reader to understand a sentence. Be that as it may, a skilled writer can craft a sentence that reduces these stop words and still makes the message clear.

This is why it matters: With character limits and people's tendency to shy away from long content, skillfully omitting these stop words means you've created more space you can use for words that are really important (read: keywords) rather than just filler copy. Again, while this is a good tip, your number one priority is writing compelling, easy-to-understand, user-friendly sentences, paragraphs, and content.

Now, don't be surprised to find (when Googling yourself in an Incognito tab) that after all the hard work you put into becoming the Hemingway of Meta Description, Google goes ahead and serves up something entirely different that the bots found on your site.

Google will do this if it believes that a different paragraph from your content offers more value and insight to the searcher.

Share Image:
Here you want to upload the Image that you would like to be presented by the Search Engine when your page is shared on social media.

Maybe this is your logo, or your Brand Image, or an Image specific to this page. Whatever it is, name it first, upload it, and Alt Text it (more on this later).

Advanced SEO:
In some website builders with a strong focus on SEO, there are additional areas where they allow you to enter even more info for the Google bots to crawl.

Things found here are best left untouched unless you want to get SEO certified to understand things like:

Custom Head HTML
Custom CSS
Inline JavaScript
Page Loaded JavaScript
And other mysteries like that.

Dammit Jim, I'm a Photographer, not a Computer Coding Engineer! Exactly. So just leave these blank if you happen to come across them, and if you don't come across them, don't worry about them.

One tip here that's easy and will make you look like an SEO pro is this:

If you happen to see 'Page Language' next to a drop down menu somewhere in your website builder, set that to the primary language you want your website to be displayed in (most likely English).

You may have experienced visiting a site from a different country, and Google does its best to translate it. If Google knows exactly the language your site should be in, this makes the Google bots and translating software very happy, and it will reflect in your SEO score (more also on this, later).

So, you've done all the work filling in the SEO spots in the inner workings of your website. Now it's time to write your actual content, that is, the words that people will actually see that are displayed on your web pages.

Again, your website should be more text than Imagery as this gives more information for the spiders to chew on and helps them understand your pages.

Whatever pages you choose to display, and if you choose to begin and commit to writing a blog, all of your content should focus on what you believe your Target Market Personas want to know, what they will find helpful, and what will make them hire you.

Once you have written your content, you're next going to format it in a way that is Google-friendly.

There are a few elements when it comes to on-page content:

- Headings
- Navigation
- Paragraphs
- Dividers

Here, it's helpful to think of Google like your Grade 12 English Teacher. He/she/they would reward you (i.e., give you a higher grade) if your essays had a title and your paragraphs were separated in a logical sequence with clearly marked subheadings. If you do this with your web page content, Google will reward you by giving you a higher grade (read: ranking).

In your website builder, you should be able to assign a Text Tag under a section called Text Properties. It's helpful to assign the Text Tag first, paste your content, and then move on to assigning the next Text Tag and pasting and so on, rather than going back and assigning all the text tags after.

The reason for this is that many website builders allow you to choose a specific font and font size for all of your headings and a different font and font size for all of your paragraphs. If you assign the proper Text Tag as you layout your page, you will see what its design will look like as you go along.

For each page you'll want to have a title. As mentioned above, this can be different from your Page Title. Your Page Title might be "About (Your City) Landscape Photographer (Your Name)."

Here your title is called your Heading aka your H1.

If you want to squeeze all your SEO juice, then you can craft something different here, such as:

"Your City-based Your Name Specializes in Landscape Photography"

Your H1 should be bigger and in bold, and above the fold (i.e., at the top of your page and displayed before your site visitor scrolls down, if they choose to).

Your H1 should also come before any of your Paragraph content or subheadings. If it doesn't, you'll lose points with Google.

You might want to place a short paragraph underneath your H1, or a testimonial, or an Image. Just keep in mind that this above the fold area is the most important area of your web page and most visitors (unless they like what they see or read) will not scroll down. If you place important info beneath the fold, it might never get seen.

When it's logical—that is, when it's helpful to your visitors—you will then want to break up your content using subheadings: your H2s, H3s, and all the way up to H6s as offered by some website builders.

H1s to H6s are considered hierarchically by Google in that the bots assume that your H1 contains more important info than your H2, your H2 is more important than your H3, and so on. So use your headings to structure your content accordingly.

It is essential to know here that you should only have one H1 Text Tag per page. If you have more than one H1, Google will penalize you. You can have multiple H2s to H6s. Again, use what will make the content user-friendly.

The Navigation Text Tag <nav> should only be used for the Text you are using for the Page Titles in your Menu bar, and nowhere else. If you use a Navigation Tag for a heading on your website, your SEO score will drop.

The Paragraph Text Tag <p> is used for the paragraph sections of your content. You can use as many <p> tags as you like.

Here it's worthwhile to mention that recommended content length is constantly changing.

A few years back, SEO experts advised that long content was favored by Google as long content suggested that the website contained more knowledge and was therefore more valuable to the searcher.

In today's TLDR (Too Long Didn't Read) culture, SEO experts are now suggesting that long content isn't the way to go, that searchers are more likely to value a site that can get to the point quickly rather than having to scan multiple paragraphs to find what they are looking for.

So how long should your content be? As long as it needs to be to express the information clearly.

Finally, the Divider Text Tag <div> should be used for design elements that help break up the content. Use this for Dividers or Spacers or fancy text like oversized first letters of paragraphs, and for nothing else.

This brings up the importance of whitespace, and how crucial it is for you (if you are designing your own website) to recognize that a lot of whitespace on each of your web pages is essential for your user's experience. Not only does it make it easier for your visitor to take in all the information laid out on your pages, it is currently what everyone is accustomed to when viewing a web page's design.

Alright, we've covered some of the basics when it comes to SEO and the text on your website. Now let's turn our attention to the Images on your website.

There are four areas when it comes to the Images on your website that relate to SEO.

The first is the Image file name.

As a Photographer, you are most likely familiar with the fact that digital Image files are usually assigned names along the lines of IMG_0123 when stored on your digital memory card and when entered into your computer.

You may, as part of your process, rename them in your Image organization and processing software (such as Lightroom), in a way that makes sense to you.

Prior to uploading the Images you'd like to display on your website, Images that ideally speak specifically to your Target Market Personas and will encourage them to hire you, you should rename them in a way that incorporates your keywords.

The reason for this is because the search engine spiders crawl every bit of your site, including your Image file names.

When your Target Market Persona searches "wedding photographers (your city)," "IMG_0123" or "Jack and Jill wed recep 1" will not seem like a top match to Google, and thus, Google will not list your site at the top of the SERP.

The task here is to really understand what terms you want to rank for when you name your Images. Rather than describing what's in the Image you are titling (that comes later), you want to again include your keywords and phrases as naturally and logically as possible.

For instance, you have an Image of Jack and Jill cutting the cake at their wedding reception. Instead of changing your Image title to:

man-woman-cake-cutting.jpg

you might want to use something along the lines of:

your-city-wedding-cake-ceremony-bride-groom.jpg

This way, when someone who is interested in photographs taken in your city of wedding cake ceremonies featuring the bride and groom, your Image and website have more of a chance of coming up at the top of the SERP.

To further illustrate this, let's say you are a business headshot Photographer. Rather than titling your Image:

man-wearing-blue-tie-against-gray-backdrop.jpg

you might want to use:

business-headshot-classic-pose.jpg

The reason is there might not be a lot of people searching for photos of a man wearing a blue tie sitting against a gray backdrop, and if they are searching for that, they most likely are not intending to book a headshot Session. The people searching for classic business headshot poses are more likely to be in the realm of interest in getting business headshots done in the near future.

If you look at the examples above, you'll notice a few things:

- Stop words ("a" "and" "the" and so on) have been eliminated as much as possible
- No capitals are used
- Words are separated by a dash, not an underscore, period, or comma

All of this is important for SEO.

Here as well: if you choose to use keywords, place them at the start of the Image file name.

You might also put your own name at the end of the Image title if you like. Again this is helpful if you are known by name in your industry and people are typing exactly your name into Google.

So, you've renamed all the Images you want to showcase on your site. Great work! The second area of Images and SEO now comes into play. Before you begin uploading the Images you've selected and renamed, know this:

Site speed, or the time it takes for your web pages to load before a visitor can see them, is one of the most important factors for SEO and ranking high on Google.

Again, bring it back to yourself. Do you wait for a page that takes longer than 3 seconds to load? Or do you go back to the SERP and click on the next link?

So, it's super important that each and every one of your Images is optimized for speed before you upload it.

Here are some tips from ForegroundWeb, an excellent web design service and resource for Photographers.[xlix] (Thanks ForegroundWeb!):

1. Start with your original Image
2. Find out the Image sizes your website builder recommends using, that is:
   500 pixels × 750 pixels for intro Images
   3,500 pixels on long side for hero Images (oversized banner Images at the top of a web page[l])
3. Adjust the Image size of each Image to the size it will be on your web page, then double it in size
4. If using the latest version of Photoshop CC, make sure you use their export dialog under File > Export > Export As …
   This usually outputs better results than using File > Export > Save for Web (Legacy), and absolutely better results than using File > Save As …
5. Save as JPG
6. Set Quality to approx. 65 percent
7. Save as sRGB
8. Save as 72 dpi
9. Export

After you've exported the Image check its file size. You want the Images you plan to display larger on your site to be under 300 kb, and Images you plan to display smaller to be under 150 kb.

Now open up the Image file and look at its quality at the size you plan for it to be on your website. You are a Photographer, so it goes without saying that the photos on your website must look top-notch in all areas including Image quality (i.e., no pixelated pictures).

If your Images look less than top-notch, go back and adjust the Quality percentage setting. Follow the next steps then look at the Image file size again and make sure it is still under 150 kb and 300 kb.

Repeat this process for every single Image you plan to upload to your website. Your site speed will thank you for it.

Now that you've uploaded all your speed-optimized photos, you are ready for the third area of Images and SEO: the Alt Text.

This is the text that is displayed while the Image is being loaded. Ideally, since you adjusted all of your Images for speed, the Image will be loaded and appear a microsecond after immediately when the visitor hits your web page.

More importantly, the Alt Text is for people that are visually impaired. Good Alt Text does not relate to SEO in terms of planting keywords in it. Good Alt Text relates to SEO in that Google and other Search Engines appreciate the effort you've put in to make all their users' experiences more accessible, including those that are visually impaired.

The goal here is to describe the Image itself in a literal sense and not the Image's context.

Using the examples above, while the file name may be:

your-city-wedding-cake-ceremony-bride-groom.jpg

the Alt Text might be something along the lines of:

Groom covered with wedding cake icing smiling at laughing bride beside him.

Hopefully, this brings the above Image to mind. You can picture it without seeing the photo.

Notice that we've written around the stop words as much as possible in the above Alt Text. Try to limit the stop words in your Alt Text as well.

Your Alt Text descriptions should be concise, short, no longer than one sentence, and they should be written as a full sentence that a human being can understand (i.e., using capitalization, periods, and other logical punctuation).

For the example of:

business-headshot-classic-pose.jpg

The Alt Text is where "man-wearing-blue-tie-against-gray-backdrop" would make sense. Only you wouldn't write it like that, you would write it as a sentence:

Man wearing blue tie standing against gray backdrop with arms crossed.

Again, ideally the sentence clearly paints the picture of the Image in mind even if you cannot see it.

Take time to craft your Alt Text as carefully as you write the other content on your site. Not for Google or for your SEO, but for people that need help viewing things on the web. Serve them.

Next comes Image Description, the fourth area relating to Images and SEO.

Yes, we just finished describing our Images, and yes, sometimes the terms Image Description and Alt Text are used interchangeably. The fact is Image Description is different from Alt Text.

Image Descriptions exist as text in the actual content of your web page in the form of captions or paragraphs describing the Image you're displaying. Alt Text appears only if you hover over the Image or when the Image is taking too long to load (ideally, not an issue with your site).

The Image Description is seen at all times on the body of your web page, and here you can use more than one sentence to describe the Image, and you might want to include technical details of how you shot it, *if* that appeals to your Target Market Persona.

Image Description Example:

With wedding photography, the art of capturing a great wedding cake smash comes from being able to read the Bride and Groom and sense when it's coming. Here, the Bride caught her Groom completely off guard. I love the surprised look on his face.

Maybe not our finest writing work, though you'll hopefully see that you can lead with your keywords and keyword phrases here, including what makes you good at your job and also what inspires you.

There are a couple stop words here and there because you want your content to be conversational and easy for people to read, follow along, and understand. With more time, we could probably eliminate a few of them from this Image Description.

So there you have them: the four areas of Images and SEO.

You ~~have~~ get to fulfill each of these four areas for **every single Image** on your site, if you want to improve your SEO.

Once you've completed optimizing everything you can on your site, there are several amazing resources that will tell you how you've done.

Most of these resources have a free plan level with some basic insights, with more in-depth reports and guidance for a fee.

Google Analytics and Google Search Console are completely free. Install the code Google gives you into the appropriate spot on your website. Your website builder Chat Person or Help articles will tell you how.

Google Analytics will show you your site speed, along with a plethora of other data about your site. Google Search Console will show you your site's performance, including total clicks, impressions (how many times a user saw a link to your site in search results), click-through rate (CTR), and average position in the SERPs.

Neil Patel's Ubersuggest is incredibly helpful even at the free level: https://neilpatel.com/ubersuggest

Semrush is also especially valuable at the free level. Example: one day we received an e-mail from Semrush that let us know there was an error on our website. Somehow, someway, an Image on the footer of our site, across all pages of our site, suddenly went missing. This happens from time to time in the world of the Internet, for some reason.

We never would have known this, and even when we checked our site on both a desktop and mobile device (side note, always check your site on a mobile device and tablet to make sure everything looks right and functions correctly) the Image was still there, as we were viewing a cached version.

We cleared our cache and indeed the Image was gone. NBD, we reuploaded it to our website builder, problem solved. The point is we never would have known there was a problem for a very long time if Semrush didn't so kindly let us know (Thank you Semrush!!!!) www.semrush.com

Both Semrush and Ubersuggest will give you scores for the different aspects of SEO as utilized by your website, for free.

Browseo may be our favorite tool out there. It's completely free, and when you enter in the URL to each of your web pages, it will come back to you with a display of how Google and other search engines see your page.

It will show you your H1, H2s, H3s, and if you have more than one H1 for some reason (it happens). What's more, it will show you if you have a stray H3 listed above your H1 for some reason (this also happens). It will show you the Alt Text that will be displayed and that Google indexes when it crawls your website, or if this Alt Text is missing (this happens too).

It will also show you all the links on your page in blue, and if a link is not working as it should, it will not be blue, so you'll know it's not working. It also shows you the SERP preview of your pages: Your Page Title (the blue clickable link that may be cut off) and your Meta Description (the paragraph underneath it that Google may have replaced with something else it found on your site). In short, the team at Browseo came up with a genius service that you can use (Thank you Browseo!!) www.browseo.net

Even though the brilliance of Browseo exists, once you've completed your website, you ~~have to get to~~ need to go through and check every page, every link on every page, and every button on every page to make sure it's doing what you would like it to do. And then you get to do this on a phone and tablet. If anything's broken, go back and fix it.

More importantly here, you want to experience your page as a visitor experiences it, especially your Target Market Persona, and ensure that all your efforts have created a superlative user experience for them.

Now before you get carried away with analytics, the only metric you need to measure is leads that actually book you. It doesn't matter if you are number one on Google, and one million people are visiting your site if not one of them hires you.

So your content must persuade them to learn more, enter your sales funnel, and your sales funnel must be able to close these leads.

As the saying goes, Google can lead the horses to water, but it can't make them drink. Maybe that's not the exact saying, though hopefully you get the point.

A few (almost) final words on SEO: Google loves websites that are consistently updated with fresh content. Think about it: what will the bots prefer to serve up to the searcher: a site that hasn't been touched in years and therefore in Google's eyes no longer relevant or a site that keeps adding and updating content constantly?

So once you're done with building, designing, and optimizing your website, realize that you are never done, and make a schedule for when you will update your content and Images, whether it's weekly, monthly, or quarterly.

ChatGPT

We wrote "almost" final words on SEO, as the preceding section focused primarily on Google, and we felt it was important to address ChatGPT as it gains popularity as a search engine. We typed in a quick "prompt" ("any form of text, question, information, or coding that communicates to AI what response you're looking for"[li]) and have copy-pasted the result:

Prompt: "Hi! What would your recommendations be for a Photographer wanting to show up in ChatGPT searches?"

Response: "Hi there! If you're a photographer looking to improve your visibility in ChatGPT searches (and more generally in search engines), it's important to approach it with a strategy that focuses on search engine optimization (SEO), relevant content creation, and leveraging your social presence. Here's a breakdown of recommendations tailored for photographers:

1. **Optimize Your Website for Search Engines (SEO)**

- **Keyword Optimization**: Include specific keywords related to your photography style and services. Think about what potential clients might search for (e.g., "wedding photographer in [city]," "portrait photographer," "best photography for events"). Use these keywords naturally in your page titles, headers, alt text for images, meta descriptions, and throughout your content.

- **Image SEO**: Since you're a photographer, your images are key! Make sure each image has:

- Descriptive file names (e.g., "new-york-wedding-photography. jpg").

- Alt text that describes the image with relevant keywords (e.g., "bride and groom at sunset, New York wedding photographer").

- **Mobile Optimization**: Many people browse on mobile devices, so make sure your site loads quickly and is responsive across all screen sizes.

- **Local SEO**: If you're targeting a specific geographic area, optimize your site for local searches. Claim your Google My Business listing, and ensure your address, phone number, and service area are consistent across all platforms.

2. **Create and Share High-Quality Content**

- **Blogging**: Start a blog and regularly post about topics related to photography. This could include things like tips for clients (e.g., "How to Pose for Photos"), behind-the-scenes content, or stories about your recent shoots. This content can rank in search engines and drive traffic to your site.

- **Tutorials and Educational Content**: Photographers can build authority by teaching others about photography. Consider creating "how-to" content that could attract people looking to improve their photography skills. Topics could include shooting techniques, lighting setups, or photo editing tips.

- **Portfolio and Testimonials**: Regularly update your portfolio with fresh, high-quality images. Display client testimonials prominently, as this adds credibility and can help with local SEO when people search for your services in your area.

3. **Utilize Social Media & Online Platforms**

- **Social Media Presence**: Regularly post on platforms like Instagram, Facebook, and Pinterest (great for photographers!). Share your work, but also engage with your followers by commenting, sharing stories, or posting interactive content. Hashtags are key—use location-specific and niche photography hashtags to reach a targeted audience.

- **YouTube or TikTok**: Short videos showing your creative process, behind-the-scenes looks at shoots, or tutorials can be a big hit. Both platforms have strong discoverability, so you can reach new audiences.

- **Online Photography Communities**: Participate in photography-related forums or platforms such as 500px, Flickr, and Reddit's r/photography. These communities can increase your visibility and connect you with potential clients or collaborators.

4. **Leverage Google My Business & Reviews**

- **Google My Business (GMB)**: Set up and optimize your GMB profile. This will help you appear in local search results when people search for photography services near them.

- **Online Reviews**: Encourage clients to leave reviews on your Google My Business page, Yelp, or other relevant platforms. Positive reviews boost your credibility and local search rankings.

5. **Use Schema Markup for SEO**

- **Photo Schema**: Adding structured data to your website, especially for images and services, can help search engines better understand your content. For example, use the 'schema.org' markup for images and services (like pricing, availability, and descriptions).

- **Event Schema**: If you're promoting a photography event, such as a workshop or exhibition, use the Event Schema to ensure your event appears in search results with rich snippets.

6. **Engage with ChatGPT & Other AI Platforms**

- **Share Knowledge**: On AI platforms like ChatGPT, you could engage in photography-related discussions, share tips, and even offer brief consultations in response to photography queries. This helps build your brand as an expert and may help increase visibility when people search for photography advice or services.

- **AI-Assisted Content Creation**: Consider using AI tools to assist with writing blog posts, creating social media captions, or generating ideas for photography tutorials. These can save time and help you consistently produce high-quality content.

7. **Collaborate with Other Creatives**

- **Partnerships with Wedding Planners, Venues, or Event Organizers**: Collaborating with other professionals in related industries can help you tap into their audiences and expand your reach.

- **Guest Features**: Guest blog posts or podcast appearances can help you build links and visibility. Sharing your expertise on photography-related blogs or websites with large audiences can direct traffic back to your own site.

8. **Use Paid Ads (if budget allows)**

- **Google Ads**: Running ads on Google targeting keywords related to your photography services (like "best wedding photographer near me") can give a quick visibility boost. You can also use Google Display Network ads to showcase your work visually.

- **Social Media Ads**: Ads on Instagram or Facebook, especially with photo galleries, can help you reach a targeted audience interested in photography services.

In summary, to increase your visibility in searches (whether through ChatGPT or traditional search engines), focus on SEO, high-quality content creation, leveraging social media, building your brand authority, and utilizing review platforms and local SEO strategies. By diversifying your efforts and consistently showing up where people are looking for photography advice or services, you'll improve your chances of standing out.

Let me know if you want more specifics on any of these!"

ChatGPT's response suggests that many of the SEO tools you've learned will conceivably help across all currently available search platforms, as well as serve as a base for future platforms. Thanks ChatGPT! (*There's no fate but what we make ...*[lii]☺)

Voice Search

Voice search is also becoming increasingly important, especially with virtual assistants like Siri, Google Assistant, and Alexa. For a Photographer, optimizing for voice search involves slightly different strategies as compared to traditional search.

People tend to phrase voice searches in more conversational, question-based ways, so adjusting your content to match those patterns is a great place to start.

Tips for optimizing your content for voice search include:

- Focusing on natural, conversational language
- Using question-based keywords
  - Voice search queries are often phrased as full questions, for example:
    - "Who is the best wedding photographer near me?" or
    - "What should I wear for a family photo shoot?"
  - Using your Target Market Personas, identify common questions they might ask about photography and create content that answers them in a natural, conversational tone.

- ○ Examples of questions you might identify and can then optimize for may be:
  - • "How much does a professional photographer cost?"
  - • "What are the best poses for family photos?"
  - • "Where can I find a photographer in [your city]?"
  - • "What is the difference between portrait and lifestyle photography?"
- • Using Long-Tail Keywords
  - ○ Searchers are more likely to use longer, more specific queries when speaking rather than typing. As such, incorporate longer, natural-sounding phrases into your website copy (e.g., "affordable wedding photographers in your city for elopement weddings").
- • Creating a dedicated FAQs Section
  - ○ One of the best ways to capture voice search queries is by creating an FAQs page on your site, as it lets you answer specific questions your Clients might have, and the content is naturally structured in a way that is easily picked up by voice assistants.
- • Being brief, but informative
  - ○ Voice search often returns concise, direct answers. When writing answers to common questions, think in terms of short, clear responses that can be spoken aloud.
- • Optimizing for Local Voice Search
  - ○ Many voice searches are location-based (e.g., "find a photographer near me").
  - ○ You can optimize for local search by:
- • Claiming and optimizing your Google My Business listing
- • Including your location and service area prominently on your website, especially on the homepage and contact page
- • Using local keywords (e.g., "Your city wedding photographer") and referencing neighborhood names or cities where you shoot
- • Using location-specific phrases in your content. People are likely to ask for photographers "near me" when

using voice search, so emphasize your local relevance in website copy, blog posts, and social media. Maybe mention nearby landmarks, areas you shoot, and specific regional photography styles.

- Optimizing for mobile and fast loading speed
  - Since voice searches are often conducted on mobile devices, make sure that your website is mobile-optimized. Google also takes mobile-friendliness into account when ranking for voice search queries.
  - As you know, slow-loading websites can harm your rankings, and this is especially true for voice search. Compress your Images and reduce unnecessary elements to ensure fast loading times. Voice search results often prioritize sites that provide quick answers.
- Adding structured data to your website
  - Structured data, like schema markup, helps search engines understand the content on your site and present it as rich snippets in search results. This is particularly helpful for voice search, as search engines often pull answers from structured data to respond to queries. For example, you could add structured data about your business hours, services, and location. This increases your chances of appearing in a voice assistant's answer when someone searches for "photographers near me."
  - Adding structured data to your Images also helps, as search engines are more likely to pull your Images in search results if they have the right metadata.
- Leveraging conversational content on social media
  - Voice search is part of a broader trend toward conversational AI. Engaging with your followers on social media through conversational posts, polls, and Q&A sessions can improve your visibility.
  - Ensure your social profiles (Instagram, Facebook, LinkedIn) are fully filled out with relevant details—location, business hours, and service offerings—since these can be pulled into search results or featured by voice assistants.

In brief, keeping in mind how people ask questions and how virtual assistants process requests while writing your content can help improve your chances of showing up in voice search results. So to speak ☺

Social Media Marketing

Here again there are seemingly endless resources on the web about marketing with social media. The good news is with all the work you did on your Target Market Personas and website content you can start with repurposing this info for your social media posts.

Examples:

- Your in-depth research on your Target Market Personas and optimizing your content for voice search will have ideally sparked some ideas for blog and social media posts.
- With the thorough FAQs page you created, you can use a social media post to let your followers know you have one and link to it.
- Those keywords and keyword phrases you spent so much time on curating? These now become your hashtags.

Like SEO and sales content, the tides and trends of what works on social media are fickle as are the platforms that are in fashion.

Your social media content will depend on your Target Market Personas and what seems to be trending at the time.

In essence, the idea is to decide for yourself how often you'd like to post (based on what is currently the popular opinion), how many hashtags to use (again based on the currently popular opinion), and when you're going to post, considering the analytics built into Meta/Instagram.

Next, you're going to come up with some ideas for additional content, themes you want to post around, categories (behind the scenes, finished work, new series, and so on), and types of posts (stories, highlights, reels, single Images, carousels, and such). Here you will decide just how much of your personal life you want to integrate, and again, all of these decisions will be based on what will appeal to and book your Target Market Personas. What do they want to see? What will they share? What will make them contact you to find out more and hire you?

Once you've decided all that, create a new spreadsheet or document and map it all out in a content calendar. Then mark the content you are posting on the appropriate date in the calendar system you are using. Then set aside some time before your first post date, and batch create as many of the posts as you can. This way you are not feeling pressured to come up with pithy, keyword-inclusive post descriptions, Image descriptions, and content as you're posting on each post day.

Again, there are analytics galore to look at in Meta Business Suite and your Instagram Business account, and again, the only metric that matters is, are people booking you?

We're at the end of this chapter now, kudos to you for sticking it through ☺

Once you've (hoed the soil, planted the seeds, watered with care) completed all of this work and your SEO is in play, you will notice a magical thing:

People will begin to contact you and out of those people, if your sales game is tight, you will book some of them. These Clients may be few and far between in the beginning; stick with it. If you're dedicated to your business, you will get better, you will improve on the knowledge you took so much time to learn and implement, and you will get more leads and book more Clients.

The marvelous part of it is this:

If you have done the proper amount and type of work in your Target Market research and created your marketing tools to appeal to them, you'll find that these exact people—the ones that will get to know, trust, and love (not just like) you and value your work—will be the ones contacting you, the ones hiring you, and the business you've worked so hard to create will begin to grow. This is a phenomenal feeling, a feeling few other things you can spend your life doing will give you.

CHAPTER 10

The Business Plan

Our work-back plan has brought us to the final chapter: the business plan.

While most business owners start with the business plan, we feel that beginning this way can be overwhelming and can lead to a lot of blank pages and looming sections to fill in.

By working backward, piece by piece as outlined in this book, you'll find that when it comes to writing your business plan, most of the hard work and heavy lifting have already been done, and your business plan is close to completion.

So why do it? You might be thinking.

Two quotes come to mind:

If you fail to plan, you are planning to fail![liii]

—Benjamin Franklin

Plans are nothing; planning is everything.[liv]

—Dwight D. Eisenhower

The meaning of the first quote from Ben Franklin is perhaps pretty clear. We understand the meaning behind Eisenhower's words to refer to the fact that things rarely go exactly as planned. It's the process of planning that helps clarify your motivations and end goals and ideally creates ideas on how to pivot as necessary.

So do it.

Do it because your business plan will become your go-to document, a house for all your goals, strategies, and ideas to live under one roof, so to write.

Do it because it will force you at this final stage to really think through your steps and ideas on how to reach your 10-year plan.

Do it because it will also make abundantly clear the areas that you need to improve on.

Do it because it's rewarding to look back at your previous business plans to see how much you've accomplished that you set out to do.

Do it because if you plan to seek funding, your investors will want to see your business plan.

Do it because if your exit strategy involves selling or transferring your business to someone else, your business plan will neatly explain everything to them.

This brings us to the next point. While your master business plan may very well be upward of one hundred pages, once you start working in and on your business (two different things), you will be busy with other things and may not have time to rework it annually.

You should, most definitely, review it annually. However, once you have your master plan, any updates or changes can now exist in a point form short-form document that outlines your goals and strategies for the upcoming Quarter.

After creating your master business plan, it is wise at this point to also do a short-form quarterly plan. You'll soon learn that things can change quickly, and ideas or marketing strategies that you hoped would take off like gangbusters fall flat or fall out of fashion, and it's back to the drawing board. Working quarterly at this point allows you to quickly pivot for the quarters to come. And when, at the end of the year, you look at your master business plan, you can make sure your mini-plans are copacetic with, and leading you to, your 10-year goals.

Writing, reviewing, and updating your business plan, and creating your quarterly plans are what's called working *on* your business. Working *in* your business includes activities such as responding to e-mails, scheduling blog and social media posts, updating your website, and so on.

Both are important, though working on your business is more important, as without ensuring that your goals are still relevant and that these daily activities are leading you to your goals, then all the things keeping you busy on a daily basis are all for naught.

Okay, here we go, Elements of a Business Plan:

Executive Summary

In the same vein as this entire book, we recommend you write this first section last. The reason for this is that the Executive Summary sums up, ideally in one page, all of the goals and strategies to reach the goals you have in mind.

The idea here is that the Executive Summary is for busy executives, and investors who will read only the first page, and will decide if they will read the rest based on its content.

It might be easier for you to write this Summary last. At the very least, it will save you time, if in case you come up with new or different strategies in the course of writing your business plan that you will then have to go back and change/update/fit into your one-page Summary.

Company Description

Here you describe your Company: who owns it, who runs it, how many, and what type of employees you have or foresee having.

Describe if you are a Sole Proprietor, S Corp or LLC, and if you are currently one type, whether you eventually plan to become another. As you will have noticed, this book does not go into the different types of business structures and the one that might be best for you. Your bookkeeper or accountant may be able to provide you with some guidance here. If not, it's wise to consult a lawyer or business management specialist as they will best be able to advise you on the appropriate structure for your own company.

Vision Statement

Remember your 10-year plan you hopefully enjoyed dreaming up? Here you will craft those dreams into a short, big-picture paragraph that expresses your vision of the future and the impact your company will have on the world. This vision statement sums up your trajectory and serves to build loyalty among Clients, employees (as applicable), and stakeholders, because ideally, they believe in your vision as well. At the very least, having this statement for you alone to reference will encourage you to stick with it for the long haul during the times that you need it.

Mission Statement

Remember all that great stuff you came up with for your brand pyramid and promise? Here you will distill all those ideas into a brief statement that summarizes what your company does, the purpose for your company's existence, the overall goals you want to achieve, and the values your company stands for. Having this succinct statement will help Clients, vendors, employees, and future leadership (if applicable) understand your priorities and what makes you unique, and ideally create a connection with them. It will also act as a touchstone that will help you respond to change and make decisions that align with your core reason for being.

In essence, your Mission Statement focuses on the present and immediate goals, while your Vision Statement looks ahead to the future.

Current Market Analysis

If you haven't done a recent Google/ChatGPT search on the state of the photography market, do so now, and summarize and reflect on your findings and how they apply to your business here.

Competitor Analysis

All that great work you did in your Target Market Persona tasks in Chapter 6? Copy-paste what you came up with when looking at your competition here and improve upon it, if necessary.

SWOT Analysis

- What are your Strengths?
- What are your Weaknesses?
- What are your Opportunities in the current market landscape?
- What are the Threats (biggest competitors, technology, economic trends, and so on)?

Target Market Personas

Here you will concisely sum up all the info you discovered during your Target Market Personas research. In a paragraph or two, describe each of your Personas, who they are, where they are, and what problems you solve for them.

Products

Here you will list and describe all the products and services you plan to offer now and in the future. Explain your products and services history (even if brief) and include a picture of the future.

A savvy business owner knows that offering a variety of products and services (aka: diversifying) is key to a successful and sustainable business. If one market or interest in one product dries up, you are not out of business.

If in figuring out your pricing you're clear on all the products and services you will offer and the revenue streams you will manage, list them here and, if necessary, improve upon them.

If done correctly, you will have thought about them from your Client's perspective. You will know exactly how your product benefits your Target Market Persona.

For products and services you plan to offer in the future, include your ideas on Product Development.

It is worth mentioning here that a qualified bookkeeper or accountant or a business manager will be able to guide you through the process of charging sales tax on tangible products (e.g., prints) if you plan to sell them. It is extremely important to seek out and implement this advice and to include this in your COGS.

Pricing Strategy

Here you will copy and paste all the work you did on your pricing. Look at it again and, if necessary, improve on it.

Product Distribution

Here you will describe how you will distribute your products:

- How will your Clients receive their Images: online Galleries, a thumb drive, or some other way?

- How will your Clients receive their prints: drop-shipped by the manufacturer? Hand-delivered by you?

If you haven't yet thought about this, do so here and fine-tune it.

Value

Here you will clearly describe the exact value you provide to your Clients, and why people will hire you above anyone else. Ideally, you will have already figured it out. Here you will crystalize your reasons why.

Branding

All your work on your USP, your Tag Line, your colors and fonts and tone: copy and paste it here and, if necessary, improve on it.

Brand Touchpoints and "Woah" Factors

List them here, and yes, you got it: improve as necessary. We'll stop writing this as it hopefully goes without saying for each and every subsequent section.

Marketing

Here you will list out your Marketing Math, along with all the marketing platforms and tools you plan to use.

Include your ideas on how you will enter the market and gain a customer base. Describe your strategy for business growth and acquiring new leads.

Develop a varied and diverse marketing tool kit, as again, you never know what's going to work. Clearly describe the marketing strategies you will employ, your budget for each tactic, your hoped-for ROI, and the system you will use to measure their success, based on your Marketing Math.

Sales Pipeline

Here you will include your Sales Funnel and closing techniques.

Operational Plan

Here you will outline the operations of your business on a day-to-day, weekly, monthly, quarterly, and annual basis.

List things like your location, hours, times you will set aside for reviewing, planning, and bookkeeping.

By creating your operational plan, you can ensure that every essential process in your business is as effective, efficient, and smooth as possible.

Organization and Management

Here you will name the main players in your business:

- Who are the owners?
- What percentage of the business does each person own?
- Who manages each aspect?

As you go about considering and completing the tasks touched upon in this book, you'll most likely come to realize that running a photography business requires a lot of time and effort and it involves many different aspects.

While it's possible for the Photographer to handle each and every component, this will affect how much time can actually be spent shooting, which will, in turn, affect everything else.

If you are a business of more than one at the onset, clearly describe each party involved in the foundation of your company, so that everyone knows their role and what they are responsible for.

If you plan to bring others on to fulfill the other roles in the near or far future, come up with your dream team of players here. Outline exactly the tasks you expect them to be responsible for, and how much you will compensate them for completing said tasks.

If you do so choose to bring in others, or outsource tasks, we highly recommend performing these tasks first to get a working-hand knowledge of what is involved. This will help you understand what your employee needs to fulfill their responsibilities effectively, the challenges they will face, and remove any ignorance on your part if duties remain unfulfilled for whatever reason the employee might give you.

Create a diagram that showcases your organization's structure, both now and in the future.

Financial Projections

Based on your Marketing Math, do your best to estimate how much your business will earn over the following 5-year span.

Establishing these projections can provide motivation and help you strive to meet a concrete goal and benchmarks to measure against instead of merely waiting to see what transpires.

Map out your Cash Flow, and think about the flow of money in and out of your business on a daily basis.

If you plan to seek outside funding, your potential investors will want to see a detailed Cash Flow, Profit and Loss Sheet, as well as a Balance Sheet. Work with your accountant or bookkeeper on these documents to make sure they are professionally laid out according to industry standards.

As we continue to cover the basics here, essentially a Profit and Loss Sheet details how much money your business earns or loses monthly, quarterly, and annually.

A Balance Sheet provides an overview of your company by listing its assets (item(s) of value owned by your company, such as equipment and vehicles as well as intellectual property), liabilities (amounts owed by your company, such as business loans, salaries, and taxes), and equity (your business's value after subtracting your liabilities from your assets).

Funding Projections

Even if you are only investing your own money into your own company, determine the amount you'll need to fund your strategies and plans. This will be helpful in prioritizing your spending while documenting it properly.

Consider your O&GE, your estimated COGS (though remember, COGS will only be expenses as long as you have made sales), as well as the costs associated with your marketing plan materials, and hiring additional employees, either now or in the future.

Clearly define your exact funding needs, how you plan to use those funds, and also how and when you will pay them back.

It's wise to factor in a contingency here that sits untouched and can be put toward investment repayment after certain milestones have been reached.

Figure out your ideal funding terms: interest amount, length to pay back, and schedule of payments due.

Understand that 20 percent to 40 percent of the total amount is usually expected by banks and investors to be provided by the business owner.

Also understand that bringing in outside investors can add additional stress while you are building your business. If at all possible consider the bootstrapping technique:

Bootstrapping "is a term used in business to refer to the process of using only existing resources, such as personal savings, personal computing equipment, and garage space, to start and grow a company"[lv] (thanks Shopify!).

Essentially, a bootstrapping business owner starts with what they have and can afford. Only when enough money is earned to pay for the next step (e.g., piece of equipment, marketing strategy, larger office, additional employee) does this next step take place.

While this strategy most likely lengthens the time for your company to progress, it brings with it the relief from stress of owing outside parties, ensures your company is 100 percent owned and built by you, and provides a rewarding feeling of satisfaction each time a new step has been accomplished.

Conclusion

Now, at long last, it's time to put your plan into action, or more than likely, you've been working in your business while going through the stages in this book and working on your business.

Either way, once your business plan is complete, if you can bring it to a business adviser, banker, lawyer, and accountant or bookkeeper to look over, do so.

This is a great place to mention that while the world we live in today provides the opportunity to learn as much as we want about anything and everything under the sun, including building a business, it is wise to find a trusted and experienced adviser.

This mentor-like figure does not have to be in the photography industry, though they should have experienced success in business. When you're working hard and have your nose to the grindstone, it's sometimes difficult to see opportunities to improve or obstacles that are holding you back. This is where having an outside pair of eyes and clear mind can help you.

Once your business plan is complete, keep it accessible and refer to it throughout the year(s) at the times you defined in your operational plan. Keep your goals clearly in sight, track your progress, and adjust as necessary. Create your short-form quarterly plan at the end of each quarter based on your current results and master plan, and keep all these plans in one place so that you can immediately see all that you've accomplished.

(If you would like a copy of our Business Plan Outline and/or Quarterly Business Plan Outline in Google Docs or Word format, please e-mail us at: natasha@markmaryanovich.com with the subject line Templates, and we'll be happy to send one along!)

So you've completed the daunting task of putting together a business plan for your business: Congratulations, excellent work!

Now is a good time to emphasize the importance of organization to a business owner. A place for everything and everything in its place is a good motto to keep in mind. Staying incredibly organized will save you time and anxiety. Knowing exactly where an invoice, receipt, or marketing post Image is when you need it frees up your time, energy, and its effect on your mindset as days turn into years running your business cannot be overstated.

All the documents, spreadsheets, touchpoint e-mail templates, sales scripts you've completed: get them organized and stay organized, you will love yourself for it.

This brings us to the importance of systems. Perhaps every giant corporation that has experienced massive success has created and implemented a system for almost everything pertaining to the operation of their business. This especially holds true for franchises.

If you've ever worked at a fast-food restaurant, you're familiar with the checklists or instructions you were given regarding how much of the frozen bag of French fries goes into the deep fry basket, how long the French fries cook for, how many pickles go on a single cheeseburger, and so on.

Or maybe you've used a gas station restroom while on a road trip and noticed the checklist on the clipboard next to the door detailing who's responsible for that day's cleaning and the duties they have or haven't performed. (Hopefully, they've performed them all.)

If you haven't seen the movie *The Founder* with Michael Keaton about McDonald's, you might want to give it a watch. At one point there is a scene where the characters draw chalk outlines of the restaurant's kitchen on parking lot cement, and they go through the motions of the employees at each station. They time the process of assembling a hamburger and are able to see when and where employees will get in each other's way. This is an example of planning out your systems and then systemizing them.

Systemize everything you can.

While this will take time in the short run, it will save you much more time in the long run. Plus, by systemizing everything from the start, you will have created the basis for your operations manual, a document that outlines clearly exactly how you want all of your procedures to unfold, a document that you can then pass along to your employees (as applicable) or as part of your exit strategy (also as applicable). If nothing else, it provides a guide for you to reference if your own memory needs refreshing.

At this point, we feel it's worthwhile to mention one last spreadsheet you might want to create: Your Flash and Sales Report.

You might want to begin a brand-new spreadsheet for this, and here you will create two separate sheets:

1. Your Outreach for the current year
2. Your Top Sheet Report for the current year

In the Outreach sheet, you will select Page Layout in the View Tab and on each page you will enter in the dates of each week of the current year.

Moving vertically beneath the week date, you'll list each date of the week, and the outreach and follow-ups you performed each day.

By keeping a tally using Excel's mathematical formulas, and creating columns for the amount of responses, shoot and rate requests as well as bookings, you will have an accurate metric of your work and the results of your work. Like so:

Table 10.1 Sample Outreach Spreadsheet

Week Date Range E.g., January 1st–January 7th	January 1st	Response Date	Total	Response	Response Rate	Shoot/Rate Request	Lead Interest Rate	Bookings	Conversion Rate
25 e-mails to new leads sent Lyle Lead responded: copy-paste his response: "Hi, I'm Lyle Lead, what's your pricing like?"		January 2nd	25	1	1/25 = 0.04%	1	1/25 = 0.04%	This column is ideally filled in when Lyle pays his advance	1/25 = 0.04%

Week Date Range E.g., January 1st–January 7th	January 2nd	Response Date	Total	Response	Response Rate	Shoot/Rate Request	Lead Interest Rate	Bookings	Conversion Rate
25 e-mails to new leads sent Lily Lead responded: copy-paste her response: "Hi, I'm Lily Lead, do you do Family Portraits?"		January 7th	25	1	1/25 = 0.04%	1	1/25 = 0.04%	This column is ideally filled in when Lily pays her advance	1/25 = 0.04%

In the Top Sheet Report, you will also use the Page Layout View and enter the dates of each week of the current year. Again, moving vertically underneath the week date you will list:

- Your cash on hand
- The balances of your bank account(s)
- The invoices receivable in the current week
- The bills you have due in the current week
- Your social media followers in each platform
- New e-mail newsletter subscribers that have joined
- The tasks you need to complete during the current week
- The sales you made during the current week. How you determine a sale is up to you. We like to list them as soon as the advance has been received, as "counting chickens before they hatch" (don't do it) is a very wise metaphor to run your business by.
- The Image Galleries that have yet to be delivered to Clients, that are then marked as delivered once sent, with the date they've been delivered
- Incoming Leads: that is, leads that you have not outreached to, and have found you ideally through your kick-ass SEO or WOM (Word of Mouth): Clients sharing their "Woah" moments with you to anyone and everyone who will listen
- Repeat Client Session requests
- Referrals that have contacted you or will be contacting you as the Referring person has let you know
- An overall tally of the leads gained within the month
- Your SEO analytics and rankings if you so choose to track them

The purpose of this spreadsheet is to really clarify the only data you should be tracking: how many leads are booking you and how many sales are you making while keeping tabs of your cash flow on a weekly basis.

How you list these elements is up to you, what makes sense to you, and is the most efficient way for you to keep track of and scan this information in a "flash" ☺

(If you would like a copy of our Flash and Sales Report Template in Google Sheets or Excel format, please e-mail us at: natasha@markmary-anovich.com with the subject line Templates, and we'll be happy to send one along!)

You might want to keep each year's Outreach sheet and Top Sheet Report within the same Flash and Sales Report spreadsheet so that you can easily compare your work and results throughout the years.

This tool provides a good summary that will help keep you focused on a weekly basis. And while on the topic of summarizations…

To sum this all up:

Create a system to keep meticulous records for everything pertaining to your business, develop an operations manual, and build a diverse group of Clients. With these basics in place, you will increase your company's chance for success, and you'll also make it attractive to outside parties, if this is part of your exit plan.

Bringing it back to the beginning:

It is extremely important these days to learn as much as you can about the business side of things, as in this digital era, it is a market crowded with Photographers. Any skills in business pertaining to following up with Clients, meeting and exceeding their needs, promotion, budgeting, and cash flow will put you over the top.

Along those lines, professionalism is the most important aspect in maintaining a successful photography career. Your Clients must enjoy working with you and enjoy the experience but most importantly, they must know that they can rely on you to show up with your best game for the job, be an utmost professional, and deliver (at the very least) what they expect.

Afterword

Congratulations! You made it through to the end of this book, and you're probably thinking: Great, thanks Natasha and Mark, you've just given me weeks/months/years of work to do.

Yes, it's true. We've left you with all the heavy lifting, and this is because no one can create your 10-year plan, determine how many Photoshoots you want to book each month, and subsequently who your Target Market Personas will be, what sales techniques work best for you, and the kind of content you want to post on social media. No one can determine any of this but you. If you do want someone to tell you how much you would like to work, for how much, and for whom and how, this is called getting a job, not running a business.

What we can do is offer a few final words to keep in mind:

If you don't want to do all that's required to build a photography business, then take photos for your life, not your living.

Life is a game of inches. The big opportunities and victories are few and far between. It is the small actions on a daily basis that create these big moments, and it is exactly these small moments that make up the vast majority of your life. So be present to them, embrace them, and recognize how important they are.

This leads us to: Celebrate the small victories.

We think the best explanation of why burnout occurs is that it occurs when the perks or rewards do not match the continuous effort put in. For most people, if they are enjoying rewards meaningful to them (e.g., a sales funnel that brings in their target goal more consistently, allowing them to enjoy dinners out, new clothes, a new car, and so on; systems in place that allow them Sundays off to spend with their love ones; Clients that appreciate them so much they constantly shower them with praise and compliments), then burnout never becomes a factor. So reward yourself when you deserve it. This will keep you going.

And if you want to keep going beyond just the basics, as we've mentioned, there is an endless amount of resources online that delve deeper into every aspect touched upon in this book. If you'd like to learn more, definitely check out the ShootProof blog (www.shootproof.com/blog) and PPA articles (www.ppa.com/ppmag/business).

One of our favorite quotes comes from the movie *Office Christmas Party*. Tying into the point about burnout, we recommend having an office Christmas party every year, even if you don't literally have an office, or if you are a company of one, or you don't celebrate Christmas. Take some time to have fun and enjoy the holidays.

Back to the quote. It can be found on a sign hanging in Olivia Munn's character's office and reads something along the lines of:

The only dumb question is the one you didn't Google first.

Google/ChatGPT prompt everything and anything you don't understand or know how to do. It's a wonderful world we currently live in, one in which you can learn about everything you could ever want to know.

Second to last point, help others. Bringing it back to Denzel Washington, who says:

The most selfish thing you can do in this world is helping someone else, because the gratification, the goodness that comes to you, the good feeling, the good feeling from helping others—nothing is better than that. Not jewelry, not the big house, not the cars; it's the joy. That's where the joy is—in helping others. That's where the success is.[lvi]

We think that's pretty cool advice.

Finally, be courageous and be kind.

Don't shy away from what scares you. Paraphrasing artist, author, spiritual teacher Florence Scovel Shinn[lvii]:

Walk up to fear and it disappears;
Run away, and fear will chase,
No matter how you run the race.
The more you flee, the more it grows,
Until it's all you really know.

Be kind to everyone and anyone who comes across your path. Kindness is contagious and creates a better world for us all.

Thank you for taking your valuable time to read this book, it means the world to us, and we truly hope it helps. If you enjoyed this book or found it useful we'd be extremely grateful if you post a review on Amazon. Your thoughts and ideas are tremendously appreciated and we read every review to make sure this book is as good as it can be.

With every best wish for joy and success,

Natasha & Mark

And now, we'll leave you with this:

Life is like a camera. Focus on what's important. Capture the good times. Develop from the negatives. And if things don't work out, just take another shot.[lviii]

—Ziad K. Abdelnour, Lebanese-American investment
banker and author

Acknowledgments

This book would not have been possible without the unwavering love, support, generosity, and patience of each of our families and friends, who have watched us struggle and learn (sometimes the hard way) how to go from starving artist to businessperson. Thank you for believing in us during times when we didn't believe in ourselves and for allowing us and encouraging us to stay on the path. We are forever grateful and endlessly thankful for having you in our lives.

And a very special thank you to Xina Martinez for gifting us with the act of friendship in copyediting this book. Thank you for your astounding attention to detail, hard work, and bearing with all, the, extra, unnecessary, commas ☺ With much love and gratitude.

Also, a note about the Endnotes: we used Roman numerals as a tribute to Natasha's Dad, who loved using them xxxxxxxx.

Thank you.

Photo Credits

Many heartfelt thanks to our amazing Clients,
it's an honor to include you in this book.

Front Cover Photo: Photographed by Mark Maryanovich
Subjects: The Matinee
www.thematineemusic.com

The 10 Elements: Photographed by Mark Maryanovich
1.1. Tarra Layne
https://tarralayne.com

1.2. Vanderocker
@vanderocker

1.3. Marc Jordan
Canadian Music Hall of Fame Inductee
www.marcjordan.com

1.4. Tacboy
https://wakeupmusicgroup.com
https://etboysofficial.com

1.5. The Manic Boys and Girls Club
www.TheManicBoysAndGirlsClub.com
www.facebook.com/themanicboysandgirlsclub
www.youtube.com/@themanicboysandgirlsclub
@themanicboysandgirlsclub

1.6. Noah Zacharin
www.noahsong.com
www.facebook.com/NoahZacharinMusic

www.youtube.com/@noahzacharin1304
@noahzacharin

1.7. Jason Campbell
www.jasoncampbellmusic.com/zen-piano

1.8. The Matinee
@thematineemusic

1.9. Maestro Carlo Ponti
https://carloponti.com
https://lavirtuosi.org

1.10. Clockwise from left:
1.10.1 Kyprios
https://music.apple.com/us/artist/kyprios/28448482

1.10.2 Ellen Cooper courtesy of *Pump It Up* Magazine
www.thesoundofla.com/ellencooper
www.facebook.com/iamellencooper
@iamellencooper
https://linktr.ee/pumpitupmagazine

1.10.3 Aaron Pritchett
https://aaronpritchett.com

1.10.4 Jeau James
https://jeaujames.com

Back Cover Photo: Photographed by Mark Maryanovich
Kyprios: The Money Shot
@kyprios12

Notes

i. Toni Ball, "The Wise Words of Warhol: 9 Famous Andy Warhol Quotes," Revolver Gallery, accessed December 4, 2024, https://revolverwarholgallery.com/the-wise-words-of-warhol-9-famous-andy-warhol-quotes/#:~:text=%E2%80%9CBeing%20good%20in%20business%20is,business%20is%20the%20best%20art.%E2%80%9D.

ii. "Michael Baron > Quotes > Quotable Quote," Goodreads, accessed December 4, 2024, https://www.goodreads.com/quotes/516322-it-s-not-the-instrument-that-makes-the-music-beautiful--.

iii. Stephen R. Covey, *The 7 Habits of Highly Effective People* (Simon & Schuster, 1989).

iv. "Norman Vincent Peale > Quotes > Quotable Quote," Goodreads, accessed December 4, 2024, https://www.goodreads.com/quotes/4324-shoot-for-the-moon-even-if-you-miss-you-ll-land.

v. Courtney Carver, 2024. "The Story of the Mexican Fisherman," bemorewithless, accessed December 4, 2024, https://bemorewithless.com/the-story-of-the-mexican-fisherman/.

vi. Quote Investigator, "Watch Your Thoughts, They Become Words; Watch Your Words, They Become Actions," Quote Investigator, 2013, accessed December 4, 2024, https://quoteinvestigator.com/2013/01/10/watch-your-thoughts/.

vii. "Business," Wikipedia, November 1, 2024, accessed December 4, 2024, https://en.wikipedia.org/wiki/Business.

viii. "Denzel Washington > Quotes > Quotable Quote," Goodreads, accessed December 4, 2024, https://www.goodreads.com/quotes/48268-do-what-you-got-to-do-now-so-you-can.

ix. "Oprah Winfrey > Quotes > Quotable Quote," Goodreads, accessed December 4, 2024, https://www.goodreads.com/quotes/3241615-do-what-you-have-to-do-until-you-can-do.

x. Adrian Grahams. "The Life Cycle of an Acorn Seedling into a Tree," Sciencing, 2022, accessed December 4, 2024, https://www.sciencing.com/the-life-cycle-of-an-acorn-seedling-into-a-tree-12486565/.

xi. "Steve Harvey Quotes About Get Money," AZ Quotes, accessed December 4, 2024, https://www.azquotes.com/author/6360-Steve_Harvey/tag/get-money.

xii. "How Much Does a Freelance Photographer Make?" Salary.com, accessed December 4, 2024, https://www.salary.com/research/salary/

posting/freelance-photographer-salary/ca#:~:text=How%20much%20 does%20a%20Freelance,falls%20between%20%2443%2C524%20 and%20%2457%2C383.

xiii. "Cash Flow," Wikipedia, October 29, 2024, accessed December 4, 2024, https://en.wikipedia.org/wiki/Cash_flow.

xiv. Brian Britt, "Einstein's 8th Wonder of the World," CLEARWEALTH Asset Management, 2004, accessed December 4, 2024, https://www. clearwealthasset.com/einsteins-8th-wonder-of-the-world/.

xv. Rob Cockerham, "In 'n Out Burger Drive Thru Menu Prices, 2001 vs. 2020," Cockeyed, 2020. accessed December 4, 2024, https://cockeyed. com/drivethru/innout_drive_thru_menu_comparison.html.

xvi. Nikki Nash, *Market Your Genius: How to Generate New Leads, Get Dream Customers, and Create a Loyal Community* (Hay House Business, 2021).

xvii. "Pat Flynn > Quotes > Quotable Quote," Goodreads, accessed December 4, 2024, https://www.goodreads.com/quotes/7519568-the -riches-are-in-the-niches-but-the-fortune-is.

xviii. "Photography Niches," FLAUNT, accessed December 4, 2024, https:// flauntmydesign.com/finding-your-photography-niche-examples/.

xix. Dave Stachowiak, "If You Build It, They Will Come," Coaching for Leaders, 2024, accessed December 4, 2024, https://coachingforleaders. com/podcast/if-you-build-it-they-will-come/.

xx. "What is an Elevator Pitch and Why Do I Need One?" Center for Career Development Princeton University, accessed December 4, 2024, https:// careerdevelopment.princeton.edu/sites/g/files/toruqf1041/files/media/ elevator_pitch.pdf.

xxi. Donna Braymer, "How Many Apples Are in a Seed?," Harrison Daily Times, 2021, accessed December 4, 2024, https://harrisondaily.com/ stories/how-many-apples-are-in-a-seed,163904.

xxii. Colin Shaw, "The Four Things You Must Do to Keep Customers Talking about Your CX," Beyond Philosophy Creating Customer-Driven Growth, 2023, accessed December 4, 2024, https://beyondphilosophy. com/the-four-things-you-must-do-to-keep-customers-talking-about- your-cx/.

xxiii. Shameika Rhymes, "5 Ways to Use the Platinum Rule at Work," InHerSight, 2024, accessed December 4, 2024, https://www.inhersight. com/blog/culture-and-professionalism/platinum-rule.

xxiv. "Temet Nosce—A Latin Sign for a Greek Oracle?" Matrix4Humans, accessed December 4, 2024, https://matrix4humans.com/matrix- temet-nosce/.

xxv. "Matthew 7:12," YouVersion, accessed December 4, 2024, https:// www.bible.com/bible/111/MAT.7.12.NIV.

xxvi.   "Touchpoint," Wikipedia, September 27, 2023, accessed December 4, 2024, https://en.wikipedia.org/wiki/Touchpoint.

xxvii.   Nikki Nash, *Market Your Genius: How to Generate New Leads, Get Dream Customers, and Create a Loyal Community* (Hay House Business, 2021).

xxviii. Tom Murray, "Mandy Patinkin has Perfect Response to Elon Musk Using The Princess Bride Quote," Independent, 2023, accessed December 4, 2024, https://www.independent.co.uk/arts-entertainment/films/news/mandy-patinkin-princess-bride-elon-musk-b2341121.html.

xxix.   Chelsea D'Angelo, "The Essential Guide to Brand Pyramids," Brandfolder by smartsheet, 2022, accessed December 4, 2024, https://brandfolder.com/resources/brand-pyramid/.

xxx.   Will Kenton, "What Is a Sales Lead? How It Works and Factors Affecting Quality," Investopedia, 2021, accessed December 4, 2024, https://www.investopedia.com/terms/s/sales-lead.asp.

xxxi.   Adobe Experience Cloud Team, "Understanding the Difference between a Sales Lead and Prospect," Adobe Experience Cloud, 2019, accessed December 4, 2024, https://business.adobe.com/uk/blog/basics/understanding-the-difference-between-a-sales-lead-and-prospect.

xxxii.   "What Is a Whitepaper? When & How to Use One," Mailchimp Marketing Library, accessed December 4, 2024, https://mailchimp.com/resources/what-is-a-whitepaper/.

xxxiii. Daniel Hopper, "How a Marketing and Sales Funnel Actually Works," LinkedIn Pulse, 2020, accessed December 4, 2024, https://www.linkedin.com/pulse/how-marketing-sales-funnel-actually-works-daniel-hopper/.

xxxiv.   "Closing Techniques," ChangingMinds.org, accessed December 4, 2024, https://changingminds.org/disciplines/sales/closing/closing_techniques.htm.

xxxv.   "Pat Flynn > Quotes > Quotable Quote," Goodreads, accessed December 4, 2024, https://www.goodreads.com/quotes/7519568-the-riches-are-in-the-niches-but-the-fortune-is.

xxxvi.   Eric Shafer, "How Many Times Do Customers Have To See an Ad?" IndoorMedia, 2022, accessed December 4, 2024, https://www.indoormedia.com/blog/how-many-times-do-customers-have-to-see-an-ad#:~:text=Modern%20research%20believes%20that%20the,it'll%20really%20sink%20in.

xxxvii. Duncan Smith, "Why the Marketing Rule of 7 May No Longer Apply," Mindlab, 2024, accessed December 4, 2024, https://themindlab.co.uk/academy/why-the-marketing-rule-of-7-may-no-longer-apply/#:~:text=It's%20often%20said%20that%20consumers,do%20more%20damage%20than%20good.

xxxviii.   Nikki Nash, *Market Your Genius: How to Generate New Leads, Get Dream Customers, and Create a Loyal Community* (Hay House Business, 2021).

xxxix.   "Effective Sales Techniques: 7 Tips for More Consistent Sales," BDC, accessed December 4, 2024, https://www.bdc.ca/en/articles-tools/marketing-sales-export/sales/7-tips-boost-performance#:~:text=Your%20business%20aims%20to%20sell,a%20close%20ratio%20of%2025%25.

xl.   Camille Trent, "Average Close Rate for Sales with Statistics to Help You Win More Deals," Dooly Sales Data, 2022, accessed December 4, 2024, https://www.dooly.ai/blog/sales-closing-statistics/#:~:text=High%2Dperforming%20sales%20organizations%20are,stage%20of%20the%20sales%20journey.

xli.   "Marketing Publicity," Active Campaign Glossary, accessed December 4, 2024, https://www.activecampaign.com/glossary/marketing-publicity.

xlii.   "Public Relations," Wikipedia, accessed November 30, 2024, https://en.wikipedia.org/wiki/Public_relations.

xliii.   "About Public Relations," PRSA, accessed December 4, 2024, https://www.prsa.org/about/all-about-pr.

xliv.   "Search Engine Optimization," Optimizely, accessed December 4, 2024, https://www.optimizely.com/optimization-glossary/search-engine-optimization/.

xlv.   "In-Depth Guide to How Google Search Works," Google Search Central, accessed December 4, 2024, https://developers.google.com/search/docs/fundamentals/how-search-works.

xlvi.   Michelle Bali, "The Official Shopify Tutorial: Set Up Your Store the Right Way," Learn with Shopify, May 13, 2021, educational video, 1:16:50, https://www.youtube.com/watch?v=u-Qfdn44rB4&t=27s.

xlvii.   "How Many People Only Look at the First Page of Google Results?" Fire&Spark, accessed December 4, 2024, https://www.fireandspark.com/seo-faqs/how-many-people-only-look-at-the-first-page-of-google-results/.

xlviii.   Miriam Ellis, "Title Tags," Moz, 2024, accessed December 4, 2024, https://moz.com/learn/seo/title-tag.

xlix.   Alex Vita, "How to Optimize Images for Website Performance: Best Image Sizes, Compression, Tools & Testing (updated for 2023)," ForegroundWeb, 2022, accessed December 4, 2024, https://www.foregroundweb.com/optimize-images/.

l.   "Hero Image," Optimizely, accessed December 4, 2024, https://www.optimizely.com/optimization-glossary/hero-image/#:~:text=A%20hero%20image%20is%20a,that%20usually%20extends%20full%2Dwidth.

li.   "No Fate (quote)," Terminator Wiki, accessed December 4, 2024, https://terminator.fandom.com/wiki/No_Fate_(quote)#:~:text= %22There's%20no%20fate%20but%20what,line%20from%20 the%20Terminator%20franchise.

lii.   "AI Prompt," CoSchedule, accessed December 4, 2024, https:// coschedule.com/marketing-terms-definitions/ai-prompt.

liii.   "Benjamin Franklin > Quotes > Quotable Quote," Goodreads, accessed December 4, 2024, https://www.goodreads.com/quotes/460142-if-you-fail-to-plan-you-are-planning-to-fail.

liv.   "Plans Are Nothing … Planning Is Everything," Jefferson Lab Montage, accessed December 4, 2024, https://www.jlab.org/montage/ plans-are-nothing-planning-everything.

lv.   Shopify Staff, "What Is Bootstrapping? It's Definition and Uses," Shopify Blog, 2022, accessed December 4, 2024, https://www.shopify. com/blog/what-is-bootstrapping.

lvi.   Jenn Klein, "Giving is Selfish!," Inspiration, Philanthropy, accessed December 4, 2024, https://youareaphilanthropist.com/giving-is-selfish/.

lvii.   "Top 50 Florence Scovel Shinn Quotes," QuoteFancy, accessed December 4, 2024, https://quotefancy.com/quote/3031973/Florence -Scovel-Shinn-The-lion-takes-its-fierceness-from-your-fear-Walk-up -to-the-lion.

lviii.   "Ziad K. Abdelnour Quotes," AZ Quotes, accessed December 4, 2024, https://www.azquotes.com/quote/810768.

About the Authors

Natasha Martinez has worked side-by-side with award-winning photographer Mark Maryanovich over the past decade. With a strong background in marketing within the film industry, Natasha played a key role in helping Mark build and sustain a successful photography business. Her strategic approach to branding, marketing, and business development has been essential in navigating the competitive photography world. Natasha's expertise, combined with her passion for creative collaboration, has made her an invaluable partner in bringing Mark's artistic vision to a wider audience while ensuring long-term growth and success.

Award-winning Photographer Mark Maryanovich has captured an impressive variety of artists including Chris Cornell, Billy F Gibbons, Bob Rock, Chad Kroeger, Elliott Smith, and Henry Rollins.

His photographs appear as album covers and artwork for companies such as Sony, Universal, EMI, Warner Chappell Music, and Mark has been nominated four times and received two Canadian Country Music Awards for Recording Package of the Year.

Mark's commercial Clients include Gibson Guitars and Peavey Electronics, and his work has been published in *Rolling Stone* and *Billboard* magazines. Mark had the honor of providing the author photo for *Model Woman: Eileen Ford and the Business of Beauty* by Robert Lacey (best-selling biographer and historical consultant on the award-winning Netflix series *The Crown*); book cover Images for the legendary Randy Bachman's autobiography *Vinyl Tap Stories*; and Matt Sorum's autobiography *Double Talkin' Jive: True Rock 'N' Roll Stories from the Drummer of Guns N' Roses, The Cult and Velvet Revolver*.

Mark has been recognized by the prestigious *Photo Review* magazine competition with his selection as a prominent entry, and by the California art community, with his placement as a finalist in the Images from a Glass Eye International Juried Photography Show, and honorable mention in the American Icon Art Competition. Because of his work in this genre, the esteemed Annenberg Space for Photography selected Mark to be part of their slideshow exhibition *Country: Portraits of an American Sound*, which celebrates the pioneers, poets, and icons of country music.

Mark's Images stand out from the masses with a unique quality, a quality created by a unique style of shooting, an experience that captures the raw essence and beauty of his subjects.

Currently, Mark is excited to be working on The ART of GIVING with cocreator Matt Sorum. Purely a project fueled by passion, The ART of GIVING exists to create awareness for the charitable causes championed by the world's most iconic artists.

https://markmaryanovich.com

Index

www.ingramcontent.com/pod-product-compliance
Lightning Source LLC
Chambersburg PA
CBHW061323220326
41599CB00026B/5001